EXCEL
EXPONENTIALLY

**Achieving Extraordinary Success Without
Losing Your Happiness, Peace, And Freedom**

By

TROY BUTTERFIELD

Published by Leadership Books, Inc. Las Vegas, NV – New York, NY
LeadershipBooks.com

ISBN
Hardback: 978-1-965401-80-4
Paperback: 978-1-965401-81-1X
eBook: 978-1-965401-82-8
Workbook: 978-1-951648-94-7

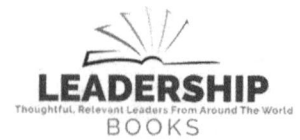

LEADERSHIP
Thoughtful, Relevant Leaders From Around The World
BOOKS

Dedication

Dedicated to my family who I hope Excel Exponentially in all phases of their lives. Also, to the "ordinary" people who are "extraordinary," but might not know it yet, but who want to Excel Exponentially.

Acknowledgments

First and foremost, I acknowledge God who is my Heavenly Father and His Beloved Son Jesus Christ for their help throughout my entire life, granting me experiences and inspiration to write this book. All glory go to them.

Second, I sincerely thank Lanelle Butterfield, my wife, for giving me her blessing and support, allowing me this opportunity to write a book. Also, I express my gratitude for my immediate family, especially my four children Zackary, Tyson, Caden, and Bridger.

Many thanks for my parents, siblings, and their families.

I would like to thank the following people for their contribution and help with this book. Some played major roles while others made minimal contributions, nevertheless all were contributors:

Troy Anderson (Inspired Literary Group), Thomas Williams, Leadership Books, Dave Hawkes (graphic designer), Tony Hanks, Raymond Johnson, Darin Murdock, Kirk and Blenda McGary, Julie Morrison, Neighbors, Friends.

My sincere apologies if I left anybody off the list.

Table of Contents

INTRODUCTION

Rethinking the Meaning of Excellence

If you are like me, you may have been educated to think of excellence as superiority or eminence. These are typical dictionary definitions of the word, along with a few others such as greatness or supremacy. Thinking of excellence in terms like these leads us to judge one's excellence by achievement of wealth, fame, high position, or power. But when we think it through, we quickly realize that these attributes do not necessarily equate with excellence. They may be the result of excellence in one's life—or they may not be. We all know that wealth, fame, position, and power are often achieved by less honorable means than through the pursuit of excellence.

What this tells us is that wealth, fame, position, and power are not valid definitions of excellence; they are merely *possible results* of excellence. But not the only possible results by any means—and as I will show you in this book, certainly not the most desirable results. It is almost a universal principle that no one who pursues wealth, fame, position, and power finds contentment when they achieve them. This means they are, of themselves, inadequate pursuits, not worthy of the expenditure of energy required to achieve them, and certainly not valid goals in the pursuit of excellence. They do not necessarily reflect excellence.

What Does It Mean to Pursue Excellence?

So, the question remains, what do we expect to achieve in our pursuit of excellence? To answer, let's push on to the heart of the matter: what is it that everyone on the Earth really wants? You may reply that there is no one answer to that question. Every person on the planet values something different from everyone else. Some want pleasure, some want security, some want success, and some want love above all other goals. But when you boil it down to its essence, I am convinced that everyone ever born wants joy, peace, happiness, freedom, and contentment. It's true that each of us will fill those words with different contents, but in the end, I'm convinced that these words summarize the deepest desires of all people everywhere.

This means rethinking a common myth that deceives many of us as we begin our pursuit of excellence. That myth is that some honorable occupations or careers are more worthy of our pursuit than others. Please read me carefully here: By *honorable* occupations and careers, I simply mean those that are honest and benefit society in some positive way. But there is an unfortunate tendency to place a higher value on some legitimate occupations than on others. For example, we tend to place attorneys higher on the scale than store clerks, doctors higher than plumbers, engineers higher than truck drivers. Such judgments are almost automatic with us, based on differences in income, prestige, education, or influence. But these judgments are wrong. The occupation or career that is excellent for you is the one that fits your particular talents and desires and enables you to meet your personal goals.

To explain why this is true, let us look at a famous biblical example from the pen of the apostle Paul. He wrote in 1 Corinthians 12 that God gave varying talents and abilities to each person so that, by working together, they would fill the various functions needed in the church. To illustrate the principle, he compared the church to a body, with each Christian as a particular organ in that body. Some members function like feet, some like eyes, some like ears, some like hands. He noted that there are visible members whose acts are prominent and thus receive more attention than others. On the other hand, the body has invisible parts. These are the less prominent members who do the necessary behind-the-scenes work that few people notice. Next Paul recognizes our common human tendency to gravitate toward the more visible, prominent roles. Then he states the obvious conclusion: If everyone were an eye, how would the body hear? If everyone were a hand, how would the body walk? The great diversity of talents and abilities is necessary for a functioning church.

Now let us apply Paul's illustration to society as a whole. A city, state, or nation could not function if everyone aspired to be governors, mayors, doctors, engineers, or lawyers. Cities and states cannot operate without electricians, plumbers, truck drivers, farmers, yard workers, salesclerks, businessmen and women, artists, musicians, etc. It seems apparent that each person is born with—or perhaps early in life acquires—abilities and interests unique to him or her—abilities that differ from those of anyone else. Not all—in fact, I would say very few—of those abilities lead to prominent or prestigious positions in society.

Now here is the sad thing that often happens. When choosing a vocation, a person endowed with a non-prominent talent that he or she loves to exercise may abandon that talent in favor of a career that earns more money or achieves greater recognition. All too often this decision is encouraged—or even almost forced—on the person by parents or peers.

I know of a boy who loved music from childhood. He became a superb piano player and while in high school was invited to perform a concerto with a symphony orchestra. But when he graduated, he yielded to the urging of his parents who strongly encouraged him to choose a more lucrative career rather than risk becoming a musician who might never achieve fame or financial success. I don't know what happened to the young man, but I think I can say this with confidence: he did not choose a path that would result in a life of excellence—a life in which he would enjoy the rewards of joy, peace, happiness, freedom, and contentment. He chose a path that led him away from his natural, God-given talent and forced himself to expend his energy on pursuits in which he had no natural ability or interest. It is very hard to achieve excellence when you step outside your talents and interests. It is your abilities and passions that drive you forward to being the best you can be.

On the other hand, I know a man who experienced the opposite of the unfortunate musician. He was the son, grandson, and great-great-grandson of preachers. It was natural for his preacher father to want this boy to follow his heritage and become a preacher as well. But from the time he was three years old, this boy exhibited a unique talent for art. He drew all the time. Even in church listening to his father's sermons, he drew whatever the sermon topic suggested, Jesus and his disciples, Daniel in the lions' den, Ezekiel in the valley of dry bones. The boy continued to draw as he entered high school, and his father, recognizing his son's talent and interest, bought him a mail-order art course to further his ability. When the boy graduated from high school, the father tried to help him find a university with a strong art department.

This wise father set aside his desire for his son to follow in his own footsteps and encouraged him to become what he was obviously meant to be. Thus, he placed the boy's feet on his true path to pursuing excellence.

Choosing the Right Goals for You

I hope I have made the point clear. Pursuing excellence does not mean pursuing the most prominent or lucrative goal. It means pursuing the goal that is right for you—the goal that will result in your own personal joy, peace, happiness, freedom, and contentment. If you have always loved being around animals, you are not likely to find complete happiness in becoming a CPA. You should consider being a veterinarian or animal trainer. If you have always loved planting and nurturing trees, flowers, and grasses, you are not likely to be content as a corporate executive. You should consider becoming a landscape architect. If you have always loved to tinker with engines and mechanical things, you won't love sitting all day behind an attorney's desk. Choose a career in a field where you can do things you know you would enjoy, such as mechanical engineering or auto mechanics.

Excellence can be achieved in any vocation, whether you are a corporate CEO or a truck driver on Interstate 40. In fact, I am convinced that you are not likely to achieve the rewards of joy, peace, happiness, freedom, and contentment unless you *do* pursue excellence in whatever career you choose. You will find real satisfaction in what you do only if you do it to the best of your ability and continually look for ways to improve.

For example, I recently heard the true story of a man—let's call him Jack—who was orphaned early and raised in foster homes. Jack managed to graduate from high school and went to work for a nuclear power plant, first as a janitor, and then as a technician. He quickly became interested in nuclear physics and took advantage of the utility company's education program to pay for university courses. After several years of schooling at night, he achieved a degree in nuclear physics and, due to his continued diligence, was continually promoted in the company. When Jack was in his forties, he became the executive vice president of the plant and finally the president. He followed his natural interests and achieved excellence.

If that example seems a little over-the-top, as if pursuing excellence will always take you to the top of the totem pole, let me bring it down to earth a bit. Achieving excellence does not necessarily mean rising to the top of the corporate ladder or acquiring riches or fame or power. But pursuing excellence effectively will always lead to greater joy, peace, happiness, freedom, and contentment. This is because when you pursue excellence in the area of your own unique talent and passion, what you do becomes part of who you are. All parts fit together to form a unified whole. Your talent and passion are applied to your chosen vocation to the point that they are essentially wed together as an organic unit.

Pursue Excellence Now! Not Later

When joy, peace, happiness, freedom, and contentment become the goals in life, it completely changes the way we approach our early vocational decisions. I encounter too many people who think we must go through the drudgery of work so we can enjoy the life we really want in our twilight years. The famous story of the businessman and the Mexican fisherman illustrates the flaw in this way of thinking.

A doctor ordered a hard-driving businessman to take a vacation, or he would soon keel over dead. The businessman chose a small, coastal village in deep Mexico. Early the first morning, he got an urgent call from his office needing help with a critical problem. The now-uptight executive couldn't sleep. He got up and walked out on the pier to calm himself. A Mexican fisherman had just docked his small boat, which was loaded with a pile of yellowfish tuna.

"What a fine catch you've got there," said the businessman. "How long did it take to catch them?"

"Only a little while," replied the fisherman.

"Your boat is far from full. Why didn't you fish longer?"

"I have plenty of fish to support my family and give a few to my friends."

"But it's still morning. What will you do the rest of the day?"

"I play with my children, fish a little, take a siesta with my wife, stroll to the village each evening to sip wine, and sing and play the guitar with my amigos."

"You'll never get ahead that way. Listen, I'm a Harvard MBA, and I can help you make lots of money. Go back and fish the rest of the day, and by saving the proceeds you could soon buy a much larger boat, then several boats and hire more fishermen. With the increased catches, you could soon own a whole fleet of fishing boats. Instead of selling your catch to a middleman, you could sell directly to the processor and eventually open your own cannery, thus controlling the product, processing, and distribution. You would need to leave this little village and move to Mexico City, then LA, and eventually New York, where you could hire the expertise to run your expanding enterprise."

"How long would all that take?" asked the fisherman.

"Fifteen to twenty-five years."

"But what then?"

The American laughed and said, "Ah, that's the best part. When the time is right, you would announce an IPO and sell your company stock to the public and make millions."

"Millions?" asked the fisherman. "Then what?"

"Then you could afford to retire and move to a small coastal village where you could play with your children, fish a little, take a siesta with your wife, stroll to the village each evening to sip wine and sing and play the guitar with your amigos."[1]

How many people start their working life with the goal of making a lot of money so they can eventually live the life they want? How sad! Why not make it your goal to live the life you want right now? What's the point of piling up a lot of money if by the time you acquire it, your best years are behind you?

Satisfaction with your own life's goals is more important than success as it tends to be defined in our culture. I'm reminded of a poem by Linda Ellis titled "The Dash," in which she notices the way one's birth and death dates are rendered on gravestones: "Here lies John Doe, 1939—2023." As Ellis says in her poem, when one passes on from this life, what matters most of all is the dash that's placed between the years of birth and death. The dash represents the

---

1 The story of The Mexican Fisherman, which I adapted here, can be found in many places on the internet. It has been credited to Heinrich Böll, who published the story in Germany in 1963.

deceased person's full life. She ends the poem with this poignant but profound verse:

> So when your eulogy is being read, with your life's actions to rehash,
>
> Would you be proud of the things they say about how you lived your dash?

Life is too short to live your dash by anyone else's definition of excellence but your own. In this book, I want to show you how you can pursue excellence on your terms in a way that makes your dash most joyful, peaceful, happy, free, and content.

What it Means to Excel Exponentially

In mathematics, an exponent is the little superscript number placed just to the right of an alphabetic letter or another number. It is written like this: 8^8. This expresses 8 carried to the 8th power, which means multiplying the number 8 by itself 8 times, which would equal 16,777,216. Possibly the most famous of these mathematical exponents is the little superscript ^{2} placed at the end of Einstein's famous equation expressing the mathematical equivalence of matter multiplied by the speed of light squared equals energy written as $E=mc^2$. In the title of this book, I have chosen to express the almost unlimited power of excellence by thinking of excellence as being continually multiplied by itself. So, not to let Einstein get ahead of me, I have devised my own equation to express exponential excellence as E^e. The point is, there is virtually no limit to excellence. You can continually multiply it exponentially as long as you can find ways to apply it.

Throughout my career as a successful small business owner, I have carefully observed the traits of people who excel exponentially. I have found that they all tend to display certain essential elements, and over the years I compiled a list of these elements all beginning with the letter "E". In these chapters, I have fleshed them out and illustrated them with explanations and many examples that make the eternal principles embodied in them come to life in a meaningful and vivid way.

I wish you well as you embark on your journey to excel exponentially.

The Essence of the Extraordinary

"People do not decide to become extraordinary.
They decide to accomplish extraordinary things."

—Edmund Hillary

G rowing up in an average family in an average neighborhood in an average town and going to an average school, I fit into my environment very well. I thought of myself as just a plain, ordinary person—"average." I never thought I was extraordinary. I wanted to be, but I didn't think I was. Even though it's common to have these feelings that there is nothing exceptional about us, I'm convinced that, deep within everyone, there lies a desire to be exceptional. We want to be admired for something. We want to think we have something to contribute to the good of the whole. We want our lives to mean something. None of us wants to muddle through our days without making a difference.

I felt that urge within myself. I wanted to excel. I tried to excel. But you know what? No matter how hard I studied, I was still a B student. No matter how hard I practiced in athletics, I was never the team's star. Did all this mean I was doomed to a life of mediocrity? That excellence was forever beyond my reach? That fate, heredity, or God had consigned me to struggle through a gray and humdrum life of non-achievement? Would that dash between birth and death on my gravestone be saying, "Here lies another non-entity who never excelled at anything"?

Well, maybe I shouldn't say I never excelled at anything. I did take second place in the second-grade spelling bee and was president of my sixth-grade class. But somehow these spectacular achievements never made headlines in *Time Magazine*.

Despite being just an ordinary guy, I was determined that my life would not be a meaningless wandering through a wasteland of mediocrity. I knew I might not become a president, a governor, or the CEO of a Fortune 500 company, but I would do my best to build a life that made a difference and had meaning. In a word, I was determined to excel.

What could excelling mean for an "average" guy like me? Well, you'll find a clue in the fact that I put quotation marks around the word "average." The truth is, there's no such thing as an average person. Within every one of us—regardless of social status, economic level, ethnicity, gender, IQ level, or handicaps—is something extraordinary. God has endowed you with some characteristics that no one else on the Planet Earth has. We know that no two snowflakes are alike. That's also true of leaves. Go pull a few off a tree and compare them. No two are alike, ever. It's as true of people as of snowflakes and leaves; no two on Planet Earth are alike. Even identical twins are never quite identical, whether in looks, abilities, temperament, or personality. Each human who ever existed is truly unique.

God created each of us as unique individuals so that our personality or ability would reflect some facet of his nature to others. This means each of us is created to know God in some way that no one else on earth can. There is no one just like you. You have some inner essence, some way of seeing things, some ability, some personal trait that no one else in the world has. This is why each one of us is extraordinary.

Exactly what does it mean to be extraordinary? Let's begin by defining the word itself. Extraordinary is one of those self-explanatory words. Its structure makes its meaning clear. We all know that *ordinary* means "commonplace," "average," "pretty much like everything else of its kind." *Extra* means "more than," "over and above," "greater than normal." To sum it up, extraordinary means above average, uncommon, outstanding, exceptional.

Every human on Earth is extraordinary *in some way*. That "in some way" tells us there is an essence within us that needs to be identified and developed. That essence is the key that will unlock your potential to excel exponentially. Do not let that word "essence" throw you off track. I am not talking about something esoteric or mysterious; I am merely speaking of that deeply seated talent, gift, or ability that lies at the heart of who you are—a gift that you may be presently unaware of. That gift was placed in you by God himself, and you will not find your happy place in life until you identify it, develop it, and employ it as your vehicle to excellence. The fact that each of us—and I do mean each of us—has this unique gift is what makes us extraordinary in some way. Because you have this gift means you have a place to occupy, a task to tackle, or a feat to accomplish that is more within your power than in the power of anyone else. In what way are you extraordinary? What is your essence—your gift? If you intend to excel, that is what you must find out.

Some of us are lucky enough that our extraordinary essence becomes visible early in life. We are quickly drawn to a certain activity that absorbs our attention and interests. This boy is fascinated early by electronic devices, or teaching, or writing. That girl loves art, or finance, or music. If these interests do not die as the person grows but become stronger and more advanced, it is a good indication that they are pointing to the person's inner essence where extraordinary potential lies ready to spring into action.

For others, however, that inner essence may not just pop out and say, "Here I am! Develop me." It is more elusive, and finding it requires a deep search within the self. That search must be made, because identifying your inner extraordinary essence will enable you to identify your life path.

In some cases, an inner essence may remain dormant until presented with the opportunity to shine. My wife, Lanelle, is an excellent example. From childhood, her one, burning ambition was to be a wife and mother. We got married and had four boys, and she was very happy as a stay-at-home mom raising those rambunctious balls of energy. But once the boys reached a certain level of independence, we decided to invest in a property management company. We needed someone to run our new enterprise, so Lanelle took over its management. Soon she was essentially running that business on her own while I managed our other enterprise. Not only did she run it, but she also turned it into one of the top companies in that entire franchise system. Lanelle found she had a talent for business, and together we launched a few more businesses. Lanelle's greatest joy and fulfillment is still in her family, but she has also found satisfaction in developing newfound talents to their fullest potential. She has excelled exponentially.

How do you go about identifying the unique gift that lies next to your heart? There may be many ways, but I have a suggestion to help you get started. Ask yourself, "What do I want from life?" You may think that is too broad a question. Each individual will answer it in a different way. But the truth is, as I said in the Introduction, when you peel away all the layers that encrust our deepest desires, almost everyone wants the same things: joy, peace, happiness, freedom, and contentment. The land where these goals flourish is your destination. Your inner essence is the track that leads you there. Switching to another track will only take you to a dead end.

To reach these universal goals, I am convinced that every major endeavor we undertake needs to be endowed with two indispensable qualities: meaning and fulfillment. Meaning and fulfillment are necessary dynamics that move us down the track toward joy, peace, happiness, freedom, and contentment. Let us explore these two qualities separately.

Meaning: *I want to make a difference.*

We all need to feel that what we do makes a difference, that our lives have purpose. When our eulogy is read, we want our lives to have been something more than just a brief ripple in a pond that quickly regained its calm surface as if nothing had ever happened. We want our dash between birth and death to mean something.

When I speak of the need to find meaning in what we do, I am not referring only to spectacular accomplishments like curing cancer, cleaning up slums, writing a bestseller, or saving the environment. Meaning can be found in the humblest of places.

For example, Gabe Scuderi had been employed for twenty-four years at a New Jersey Lysol factory. He never thought his job was important until the early days of the COVID-19 pandemic when he came home to find his little daughter waiting for him at the door. Bright-eyed and excited, she greeted him as a hero. She had just watched the evening news and learned the vital role of Lysol spray in combating the spread of the disease. The little girl opened Scuderi's eyes to the true meaning of what he did every day. "It's the first time I felt this isn't only a job," he said. "We're on the front lines now."[2] On that day Scuderi's job became something more to him than a necessary daily grind; he now saw it as a vital link in a chain of meaning. He was part of something bigger than himself. It gave his everyday work meaning and purpose. As Pope John Paul wrote, "Man expresses and fulfills himself by working." This is especially true when his work contributes to the common good. This is what Gabe Scuderi discovered. His work was a vital thread in the interwoven fabric of society, and it gave his life a sense of meaning.

Mr. Scuderi's story tells us something important. I don't know the man, of course, but judging by his story, I'm willing to bet that he did not apply to the Lysol factory because, from childhood, he was intensely interested in manufacturing disinfectants. My guess is that he got out of school and needed a job, and the Lysol factory happened to have an opening. So, he went to work, made a decent living, and supported his family. That is all well and good. The world is filled with good, responsible people who expect nothing more from a job, and it is an honorable thing that they stick with it and support

2 Michael M. Phillips, "Lysol Factory Job Becomes a Calling. 'Hey, I Work at the Place That Makes That,'" *Wall Street Journal*, April 21, 2020, https:// www.wsj.com/ articles/the-workers-at-a-lysol-plant-have-a-mission-now -11587482618.

their families while enduring what they see as a humdrum work. But life got so much better for Scuderi when his job was transformed into a calling. It enabled him to find meaning in his vocation.

But suppose you do not find meaning in your job. You may sit in a cubicle every day doing mundane work for a company that makes widgets that do not save or improve lives. How do you find meaning in such a job? The meaning may not be so much in the company product or in the task you perform; it may be found in the way you perform your work. I remember seeing a police officer who delighted motorists with his enthusiasm by dancing and using expansive arm movements when he directed traffic. Your job may lead you to discover that your deepest ability lies in relationships. Exercising this talent may diffuse conflict and promote an atmosphere of peace and cooperation that improves the workplace atmosphere and increases productivity. In finding your gift, you find meaning. What you do makes a difference in the lives of others.

What I am saying is this: Your central, extraordinary essence may be a gift you could exercise in any job. Your job may lead you to discover that your gift is persistence, patience, meticulousness, relational skills, organizing, analyzing, or any number of qualities that can be applied almost anywhere. Applying these skills may enable you to do your seemingly mundane job in a way that enhances your life and lifts it out of the ordinary. The job you took simply because it was available becomes a source of satisfaction because it gives your unique skills a productive and rewarding outlet.

This is what happened to Raymond Johnson. Raymond was a dump truck driver employed by a delivery firm in Oklahoma City. Because he is black, his coworkers often harassed him. Once they put a dead skunk in his truck. Another time they disabled his truck's brakes, causing him to crash into a fence.

Raymond started doing some odd jobs for the property management company my wife and I owned in Oklahoma City. Because his diligence and integrity impressed us, we contracted with him to do several kinds of jobs for us on the side. Although Raymond was dealing with severe personal problems at the time, he continued to give us that consistent quality and diligence that has become so rare in workers these days.

We knew the harassment he was enduring was turning his work life into an earthly hell, so my wife offered him an opportunity to work part time for us as a vendor. He graciously declined the invitation because his employer had been good to him, and he did not want to leave the man high and dry. But after the disabled brakes incident, he realized he needed to get out of that environment. He gave his employer adequate notice and began to work full time for us as a vendor. He was doing the same work as before, but now he was running his own company, making more money, and experiencing more peace, joy, happiness, freedom, and contentment.

As you can see, it was not Raymond Johnson's truck driving skills that gave him his extraordinary essence (although those skills are indeed superb), it was his dedication, loyalty, and extraordinary work ethic. Raymond did not set out early in life to become a truck driver or a business owner. But he excelled exponentially because he discovered and developed the deeper essences that resided within him. It may not be the job itself that delivers excellence. It may be how you do the job.

Fulfillment: *I want to experience satisfaction.*

We all need to experience a sense of satisfaction in what we do. In the Introduction of this book, I told the story of the young man whose preacher father encouraged his talented son to become an artist. What gave this young artist satisfaction was successfully completing a painting. Later, when he was trying to establish his footing in a freelance studio, he went through times when he did not get enough business to support himself. To supplement his income, he decided to sell encyclopedias door-to-door. He went through the training process and set out on his alternate career as a salesman.

He hated every minute of it. He dreaded knocking on each door he approached. He dreaded trying to convince reluctant prospects to buy something they obviously did not want. When he *did* make a sale, which was rare, he felt guilt, thinking he may have manipulated someone into shelling out money they could not afford to spend. He got absolutely no satisfaction from selling.

On the other hand, some of his colleagues who went through the same training enjoyed selling immensely. They did not think they were manipulating their customers. They were simply helping them to clarify their needs and make up their minds. They looked forward to the challenge of knocking on the next door. They piled up scads of sales and got immense satisfaction from doing it.

I do not think I need to belabor this point. The artist got great satisfaction from completing a book illustration but not from selling a book. The salesmen got great satisfaction from selling but would have hated (and failed at) trying to draw a recognizable figure. Each of us is unique, and it takes all our uniqueness working together to create a dynamic society. When we find what gives us the greatest satisfaction, we have found the essence of what makes us extraordinary. We have found our path to excellence.

The Happy Ending

Pursuing meaning and fulfillment opens the door to joy, peace, happiness, freedom, and contentment. Some readers may think I have left one vital element off this list of human desires: the desire for love. I did leave it off, and the omission was deliberate. Love is not something you can achieve by discovering and utilizing your innate vocational talents, which is the primary focus of this book. But I contend that achieving excellence opens the door to nourishing love.

To demonstrate what I mean, let us return to Raymond Johnson's story. When I asked Raymond what he was doing to take the excellence he had already achieved to the next level, he said, "I've been looking to expand and have people work for me so I won't have to work so much and can take more time to enjoy what life has to offer." When pressed to explain, Raymond said that success would give him more time with family and to "help somebody that needs a job, an opportunity, or just a chance to work."

What more can I say? Love for family and love for others are the most noble of motivations to achieve excellence. Sharing that excellence with others, as Raymond did, is what makes excellence exponential.

2

Establish Your Expectations

"Let us be about setting high standards for life, love, creativity, and wisdom. If our expectations in these areas are low, we are not likely to experience wellness. Setting high standards makes every day and every decade worth looking forward to."
—Greg Anderson, race car driver

When I was a high school teenager, there was not much to do in the small town of Kaysville, Utah. On Friday nights, my two good friends and I liked to stay out late. One of them owned a pickup truck, so we often spent the evening just driving around. First, we drove up and down the main drag, looking for other friends or girls we knew we could hang out with. But as the evening wore on, business doors closed, lights went out, and the sidewalks and streets emptied. With nothing better to do and not wanting to go home, we three exemplary epitomes of time management continued to drive aimlessly about the town.

I remember one of these nights quite well. We were still moseying through the streets a little after two o'clock in the morning when the strobing red lights of a police car flashed behind us. We had no idea why we were being stopped. We were not speeding, and we never drank alcohol or used drugs. We pulled over, and the policeman came to the window. "What are you boys doing out this late?"

"Nothing, we were just driving around," our driver replied, "Why did you pull us over?"

"Where are you going?" the policeman responded.

"Nowhere," my friend replied. "Like I said, we were just driving around."

"Well, then," the policeman said, "I pulled you over for driving without a destination."

We were dumbfounded. *What?* We thought. *Driving without a destination? That's not criminal.* That was true, of course, and after listening to us trying to convince him that we meant no mischief, the policeman probably figured we were not enterprising enough to get into much trouble, so he let us go.

But when you think about it, even though driving without a destination is not criminal, it is still a pretty serious charge. To be going simply for the sake of going indicates a lack of purpose, a lack of a goal. It is a waste of time, energy, and resources. It makes no sense to embark on a journey without a destination. Games such as football, soccer, hockey, and basketball are meaningless without a goal. The same is true of life. A life lived with purpose (a goal) has meaning, whereas a life without purpose does not. Without purpose, one drifts about aimlessly like a loose dog following random rabbit trails and chasing every squirrel that crosses its path. With no destination, you just hope something interesting, useful, or worth pursuing pops up.

To avoid driving without a destination, it is vital to determine what you want in life. You do this by establishing expectations and setting goals. In this chapter, I will offer four pointers for establishing your expectations and setting your goals accordingly.

1. Set Your Expectations High

There is a scene in an old 1949 Christmas movie, *Holiday Affair,* in which Robert Mitchum helps a fatherless boy learn to hit a circle drawn on a chalkboard. The boy tries, but the ball always hits below the target. Mitchum then tells him to aim his ball above the circle. The boy does so, and to his elation, the ball strikes the circle. Mitchum explains the boy's success: "If you aim higher than the mark, you've got a better chance of hitting the mark."

It is a universal principle: To aim high and miss will put you in a better position than to aim low and succeed. It is like the basic principle of all bargaining. The seller always has in mind a figure he expects to get. But he sets a higher asking price knowing the buyer will offer a figure lower than what he wants. The high asking price enables him to meet his expectations somewhere in the middle. In setting your expectations high, you are bargaining that you will achieve a better life than if you had aimed low.

I must, however, offer a strong caution. While high expectations are highly desirable, it is wise to be sure they are also realistic. But remember, the important thing is to aim at something. Set a target and try to hit it. You may miss it sometimes, but you keep trying. As Zig Ziglar said, "If you aim at nothing, you will hit it every time."

2. Set Your Expectations Realistically

My ten-year-old son Tyson loved basketball. He was a good player, but he was not the star. One day he expressed to me his aim to someday play in the NBA. I did not want to point out that he probably lacked the skills and potential height needed to become a professional basketball player, yet I wanted to prevent his pursuit of an unrealistic goal that would lead to inevitable disappointment. So, I asked him, "Tyson, do you know how many boys from Morgan County have made it into the NBA?"

He pondered a moment before guessing, "Three?"

"Think again," I said. "The answer is zero. Of the many millions of boys that have grown up in America since the NBA was established, only a tiny fraction of a percent ever became professional basketball players."

I was not trying to pour cold water on my son's high aim; I was merely trying to get him to aim at a different target—one that would be possible for him to achieve. Unfortunately, I hear of many parents who tell their children, "You can be anything you want." That advice sounds encouraging and affirming, and it conveys confidence in your child. But it is simply not true. No one can be just *anything* he or she wants. A man who weighs 97 pounds cannot be an NFL offensive lineman. One who weighs 260 pounds cannot be a jockey. (Maybe someone should talk these two into switching goals with each other.)

Young people are typically attracted to glamorous professions like sports, film, pop music, or even politics where they see their heroes accomplishing great things or exercising great power in movies and on TV. It is not unusual for a kid to say, "I want to be a movie star," or a rock star, a model, a fighter pilot, an Olympic athlete, or a football quarterback. These dreams are almost always unrealistic, but sometimes they linger, and we find them hard to relinquish.

Notice that I said, "These dreams are *almost* always unrealistic." Let us deal for a moment with that word "almost." The rule of realism has exceptions. Every now and then, a person is born who does have the talent, intelligence, and physical attributes to achieve stratospheric expectations. The extraordinary voices of many opera sopranos became apparent in the singer's youth. Most football greats displayed aptitude and potential for size, strength, and speed on Pop Warner fields and in high school. Mozart composed symphonies before he was ten years old. Picasso was painting when he was nine. When such exceptional talent and abilities are apparent to all, then by all means, aim high at the rare target, even though it may be one that only a select few can hit. As noted above, even if you hit a little beneath it, you are still better off than if you aimed too low. In those rare cases, the exceptionally talented person may need to ignore those voices insisting that his goal is unrealistic and that he should go into a safely achievable vocation.

3. Evaluate Your Assets

When dreams of the future begin to form, how is one to decide what target he or she should aim at? Which expectations are realistic, and which are not? The answer is, do not make your decision in a vacuum; base it on what you have learned about yourself through experience. Evaluate your strengths, talents, proclivities, passions, and interests. Structure these elements into a unified whole that integrates them in ways that support, interact with, and enhance each other. Then you have the foundation for establishing your expectations.

To establish valid expectations, here are some questions you should ask yourself: Is there an activity that I am consistently drawn to do or think about consistently? Do I always enjoy the process of doing this activity? Am I good at it? Have I improved? Do I mind working out the problems I encounter? Has my deep interest in this activity lasted over a significant period of time? Am I always searching for time to engage in this activity? When I am working on it, do I pretend not to hear the call for dinner?

As you go through this process, remember that no one is ever completely objective about himself or herself. Our self-evaluation is always colored by our desires and biases and distorted by our blind spots. Therefore, as you make this evaluation, seek the advice of someone you trust who knows you well and has your best interest at heart. Run your own self-evaluation by him and draw out his observations about your strengths and weaknesses.

Here I want to emphasize what I have noted several times in this book already. Your goals need to be established solely on your own terms—based on your talents and desires. You must not look across the fence and imagine that, because the grass there appears taller and greener, it will nourish you better. If what gives you joy is programming a computer, you must not let the glamor, prestige, or potential riches of a career in, say, show business cause you to waver in making the wisest choice for your long-term well-being.

It is only after establishing realistic expectations that you can begin to build a life that will give you joy, peace, happiness, freedom, and contentment.

4. Keep Your Expectations Flexible

How do you set expectations if a strong, compelling interest does not appear in your formative years? This lack of certain life direction is not uncommon. For some, outstanding talents, interests, and aptitudes remain dormant and do not become plainly visible or identifiable. In other instances, a person may be blessed with two or three strong interests or talents and have trouble deciding which to pursue. How is one to establish expectations in such cases?

Whether or not we have established our expectations, most of us are forced to make choices about our futures when we graduate from high school. We are compelled either to choose a college major or get a job. Often the job choice is based on availability and the major is a stab in the dark. Since the choice is based essentially on the immediate need to make a decision, whether it fits you is a hit-or-miss proposition. That is why it is important to keep your expectations flexible. You may enter a field that looks attractive on the surface, only to find that the deeper you get into it, the less it resonates with your deepest desires.

My first ambition was to go into sports medicine as a physical therapist. But I was not a very good student, and it soon became clear that I would not make it in the field of medicine. At that point, my father-in-law, a successful entrepreneur, recommended that I take some business classes. He said, "Having some knowledge of business will help you regardless of what career you choose." I followed his advice and took a marketing class, and to my surprise, I found myself strongly drawn to that field. So, rather than rigidly holding onto my original plan, I switched majors, which eventually enabled me to establish my own successful businesses. Thank goodness that despite whatever shortcomings I may have, I had the wisdom to listen to my father-in-law! I now keep Gumby on my desk to remind me to be flexible when better opportunities arise.

Often unexpected opportunities pop up out of the blue, and you may find that switching from the track you have chosen will lead you to a more satisfying destination. Many people found their true calling by following opportunities that uncovered talents and interests they never knew existed until the opportunity to exercise them appeared.

The life of the iconic film director Steven Spielberg gives us a striking example that vividly illustrates much of what I've covered in this chapter. We all recognize Spielberg as a man with exceptional talent. He aimed high. And he knew early on exactly what he wanted to do in life.

It all started when Steven was six years old, and his father took him to his first-ever movie. It was the just-released 1952 Cecil B. DeMille epic about the circus, *The Greatest Show on Earth*, starring Charlton Heston and James Stewart.

Young Steven was fascinated by the enormous wreck that climaxes the film when two circus trains collide. He asked his father for two Lionel train sets for Christmas. Then he borrowed his father's 8mm movie camera and filmed his two trains crashing together, trying to recreate what he had seen in the movie. He watched his little film over and over and asked himself, "What else can I do with this camera?"

As a Boy Scout, Steven earned a photography merit badge by filming a western home movie with his siblings as actors. The scout troop loved it, and their response set a fire under him. Filming became a compulsion. He began to accumulate amateur movie equipment and soon was making little 8mm movies almost constantly, using school friends as actors.

From that time on, Steven Spielberg knew what he wanted to do with his life. He studied film at Cal State and got an apprentice position at Universal Studios. Soon he was given a chance to direct a short film that impressed the studio executives enough to offer him a contract. After his first feature films—*Jaws*, followed by *Close Encounters of the Third Kind* and the *Indiana Jones* films—Steven

Spielberg became a household name and is now recognized as the most commercially successful film director of all time.

He discovered his talent and interest early and dedicated himself to improving it. He set his expectations high and achieved them spectacularly. He followed his dream and found contentment. I will end this chapter with an appropriate bit of advice taken from a brief speech he delivered to a group of young filmmakers:

> Sometimes a dream just whispers. And I've always said to my kids: the hardest thing to listen to, your instincts, your human intuition, always whispers, it never shouts. It's very hard to hear. So you have to every day of your lives, be ready to hear whispers in your ear... And if you can listen to the whisper, and if it tickles your heart, and if it's something you think you want to do for the rest of your life, then that is going to be what you do for the rest of your life, and we will benefit from everything you do.[3]

Those whispers that tickled Steven Spielberg's heart expanded exponentially as he worked to excel at being a world-class filmmaker. In time those whispers became soundtracks that reverberated in tandem with stunning cinematic images throughout the world's motion picture theaters. I think Spielberg's example makes the point clear. When you listen to the small voice in your heart and continue to heed it despite the glittering attractions that attempt to lure you down countless rabbit trails, you will amplify that voice into one that will inevitably be heard throughout your own environment if not further. In other words, you will excel exponentially.

---

3 "From Director Steven Spielberg" https://fromdirectorstevenspielberg.tumblr.com/post/34287250670/spielberg-recounts-the-story-of-the-first-film-he

Expand Your Education

*"Education is no longer thought of as a preparation for adult
life, but as a continuing process of growth and development from
birth until death."*

—*Stephen Mitchell*

One of the most inspiring success stories of our time is that of Dr. Benjamin S. Carson. Carson was born in Detroit, Michigan, and raised in poverty by his single, almost illiterate but loving mother, Sonya. She worked two or more jobs just to make ends meet.

Anger over his circumstances and the prejudice he endured as a black student plunged young Ben into a downhill slide headed for certain disaster. By the time he reached the fifth grade, he had fallen to the bottom of his class. His failing report card spurred his mother into action. While cleaning homes for affluent families, she had seen diplomas on walls and books on shelves everywhere. She decided that education was the key to success, and reading was the key to education. She demanded that Ben and his brother check out two books per week and submit written reports on them. Though illiterate, she pretended to read the reports. She limited TV watching to three programs per week. The boys resisted, but their strong-willed mother prevailed.

Sonya Carson's stringent program turned young Ben's life around. He found that he loved reading and began to devour books voraciously. His vocabulary, comprehension, and understanding improved to the point that he graduated from high school with honors. He then earned a degree from Yale University and finally a doctorate from the University of Michigan Medical School. At age thirty-two, he became the youngest ever head of Pediatric Neurosurgery at Johns Hopkins University and gained worldwide fame for pioneering several life-saving surgical techniques. After Dr. Carson's retirement from medicine, President Trump appointed him to his cabinet as Secretary of Housing and Urban Development.[4]

Ben Carson continues to live his mother's motto: "Learn to do your best, and God will do the rest." He made no secret of the fact that he prayed for God's guidance before performing surgery.

Although Ben Carson's mother was illiterate, she understood that a master key to excelling in life is a good education. You may feel impelled to challenge her conclusion, saying you know of many people without college degrees or even a high school diploma who achieved excellence in many fields. Well, so do I. Abraham Lincoln, whose eloquence and brilliance awes us even today, had little formal schooling. Thomas Edison, the inventor of the electric light bulb,

4 Adapted from "Why Reading is Important/Ben Carson," on the website "Best Books for Kids" https://www.best-books-for-kids.com/ben-carson.html

phonograph, motion picture camera, and electric power generators, had less than a year of formal education. Both Wright Brothers managed to get off the ground without graduating from high school. Mark Twain, Henry Ford, and Michael Faraday (inventor of the electric motor, electric generator, and electric transformer) had no formal education at all. Mary Kay Ash, founder of the $1.2 billion-dollar company Mary Kay Cosmetics, had no education past her high school diploma. Celebrity TV cook Rachael Ray also made it to the top without a university education. My friend Tom, who has written more than a dozen books, all published by major publishers, has seen the inside of universities only to deliver lectures.

These achievers did not have degrees, but I contend that they were educated. Lincoln, Edison, Twain, and Faraday, like Ben Carson, were voracious readers. As a child, Edison was fascinated by technology and spent hours experimenting. Faraday, apprenticed to a bookbinder at age fourteen, constantly read the books the shop turned out. Lacking formal education, these men educated themselves, discovering and developing their interests and strengths through reading and experimentation.

Education is vital to achieving excellence, whether it comes from universities, trade schools, on-the-job training, or even the school of hard knocks. Today it is hard to get a good start in life without at least a high school diploma. That little document is a launching pad into both the world of work and institutions of higher education.

Nowadays it is common for parents to push their children toward a college education. This is an absolute necessity for success in some fields, such as medicine, law, teaching, and engineering. But it is not necessarily the best educational route for everyone. Instead of deciding in advance that college education is an absolute must, wise parents will first determine and evaluate their children's skills and proclivities. In today's world, many are finding that a university education is not always the best choice.

My wife and I discovered this fact while raising our four sons. Believing, like Sonya Carson, that reading is the key to education, we read to our sons constantly. We read picture books, story books, learning books, Bible stories, animal stories—whatever we found uplifting, informative, and interesting at their level. (You should ask about their teary-eyed experience with the book, *Where the Red Fern Grows*.) All four boys grew up loving to read, and all did well in high school. Three of them—Zackary, Tyson, and Caden—were more academically inclined, and did very well in college. Our fourth son, Bridger, however, is more of a hands-on learner. I mean that literally. He loves working with his hands, building things, and solving construction problems. Instead of entering college, we encouraged him to get a job on a good construction crew where he would be trained by the best in that profession. That is what he did, and now he is working successfully in the construction field.

As you can see, education comes in several guises. One of the most effective is experience, a.k.a. the "school of hard knocks." It has been said that experience is a tough but effective teacher: It gives the test first and the lesson afterward. I like what American businessman John Bogle said: "Learn every day, but especially from the experiences of others. It's cheaper!"

Remember that the point of education is to enable you to achieve excellence, not just to land a prestigious job or make a fortune. The key to a good education is to acquire the specific kind of knowledge that will enable you to achieve excellence both in your chosen field and in your life. In many cases, that means college is the best choice. But in our present culture, college education can pose some formidable challenges, and it may not always be the best path toward one's particular goal. A college education would have been overkill for our fourth son—like buying a tux to wear to a country swing dance.

My point so far is that while education can take many forms, it is vital to be educated in some way, or success in business and in life will elude you. With that said, I now want to make a second point, which I think is every bit as vital as the first.

Education Must Never End

Just because you have graduated, just because you've got a degree or a trade school diploma, just because you have started a business, just because your business is successful, don't think you can stop being educated. You must see to it that education continues all through your life. Unless you stay sharp and on top of what is going on in your field, you are going to fall behind your competitors.

In some critical fields, continuing education is mandatory. Though requirements differ from state to state, continuing medical education (CME) is required of all physicians in the United States. For example, in Texas, medical doctors must complete forty-eight credits of CME every two years to maintain their license to practice. The recertification for airline pilots is called Recurrent Training and includes both the classroom and the simulator. Frequency of training varies from airline to airline. Public school teachers in most states are required to take a specified number of hours of continuing education annually.

While most of us in less critical fields such as commerce, manufacturing, transportation, etc. are not required by law to engage in continuing education, I believe strongly that we must do so to maintain a competitive advantage. In today's fast-paced environment of ever-developing technology and trends, you cannot stay abreast of the times unless you stay acutely aware of the inevitable changes going on in your field and related fields. In the real estate world that I have long inhabited, there is a critical need for continuing education. One must take classes periodically to stay up to date with the changes in the industry and the law.

There is also another reason for continuing your education. Unless you broaden the scope of your knowledge in areas outside your field—knowledge about people, the past, and your world—you will become narrow and one-dimensional. You will be like a virtuoso violinist no one wants to hear because he can play only one note.

How do you make continuing education happen? How can you continue and broaden your education so that learning becomes a process that builds throughout your life? Here are a few ideas, some of which I've tried, and others I've gleaned from friends and other sources.

Find Experienced Elders or Mentors: Wise people build on past knowledge. Depending on the wisdom, achievements, and experience of those who have gone before us relieves us from the burden of learning all the basics by trial and error. The knowledge we gain from the past gives us an advantage in the race by moving our starting block much farther down the track.

Where would we be if every generation had to reinvent the wheel? Historians presume the first wheels were simply logs placed on the ground beneath heavy objects to roll them down a path. It was a cumbersome process, continually moving the logs from behind the object to the front so it could keep rolling toward its destination. Then, some bright fellow sliced the logs into disks, ran an axle through two of them, placed it under the heavy object, and pulled it to its destination with an ox. Another person came along and designed a stronger wheel using thick planks and sawed it into a circle. These wheels were stronger, but they were heavy, cumbersome, and wore out quickly until someone figured out how to make a wheel of spokes and a rim with a steel band forged around it for durability. Then, centuries later, the Industrial Revolution provided vulcanized rubber from which tires could be made to create wheels of unprecedented lightness and durability.

The same principle applies to any industry or business. After elementary beginnings, innovative minds improve techniques, standards, procedures, materials, and products to the high sophistication we enjoy today. We stand tall today because we stand on the shoulders of our forefathers. The wise person will take care to remain acutely aware of this progression of knowledge and take advantage of what has already been discovered and learned.

One of the best ways of doing this is to seek out experienced people I like to call "the elders," older people in your field who have "been there, done that." They know the ropes, the pitfalls, and the common mistakes beginners tend to make. They can call on their own experience and the experience of others to aid you in navigating the minefield of competitive business or life for that matter.

How do you find these elders or mentors? I have found that they often simply pop up in your path. The business you choose to pursue will automatically put you in contact with others in the same field, and usually out of the many contacts you make, some will be "elder statesmen" who are often willing to counsel younger people who have embarked on the path they have already trod. In fact, retirees are often looking for ways to share the knowledge they have accumulated. It adds meaning to their lives, and for them to have a mentee means mutual benefits to both parties. One of my first business mentors was my father-in-law. As I mentioned in the previous chapter, he recommended that I take some business classes until I found a career that interested me. He knew that, no matter what profession I entered, it would help me to know how business operates. As it turned out, I ended up liking marketing and advertising, which meant the business classes were extremely helpful to my career. I learned firsthand the value of having a person to whom I could go with any question and depend on getting an answer drawn from a wealth of knowledge and experience.

Speaking of answering questions, I'm reminded of a story about a grade-school boy doing his homework one evening who asked his father, "Dad, what explorer discovered South America?" The father replied, "Well, I don't know, son." A little later, the boy asked, "Dad, how do you spell chrysanthemum?" "Well, I'm really not sure, son." Several minutes later the boy asked, "Dad, what is electricity?" Again, the father replied, "I just don't know, son." Then the boy said, "Dad, do you get tired of me asking you questions?" The father replied, "Oh, no, of course not. Ask all you want. After all, how can you ever learn if you don't ask questions?"

Fortunately, most mentors are not like this clueless father. They become mentors because they *know* the answers, which are drawn primarily from their experience.

Small Business Administration Services: The U.S. Small Business Administration provides a free resource designed to mentor small businesses. The program is called SCORE Business Mentoring. According to the official website, "SCORE, the nation's largest network of volunteer, expert business mentors, is dedicated to helping small businesses plan, launch, manage and grow. SCORE is a nonprofit organization that is driven to foster vibrant small business communities through mentoring and educational workshops."

SCORE mentors offer advice at no cost in fields such as financing, human resources, and business planning. Their volunteers work with you via email, telephone, and video. All SCORE mentors are experts in entrepreneurship and related fields. They meet with small business clients on an ongoing basis, providing continued advice and support. Other SCORE services include training, webinars, online workshops, courses on demand, and a library of online resources.[5]

Other Sources for Continuing Education: Trade journals are published for almost all businesses of significant size, whether it is trucking, animal breeding, writing, construction, real estate, advertising, teaching, publishing—you name it, and there is a trade journal for it. These magazines are usually published monthly, both in print and online. They feature news of what is going on in the industry, changes in laws, and articles on specific subjects by experts in the field. Many read these journals, cover to cover, as their primary source of ongoing information about their particular industry.

As far as I know, all universities allow non-registered students to audit classes for a nominal fee. Course offerings are so varied now that it is usually easy to find courses applicable to most businesses and industries. I have an artist friend who audited an art course in freehand sketching. A writer I know audited a course in English composition. Almost all universities now offer online courses for continuing education in many fields.

YouTube and other online sources offer an almost endless variety of information in various forms, from hour-long lectures and demonstrations to short instructional videos that present highly useful and pertinent knowledge in many fields.

There seems to be no limit to the number of conferences, seminars, conventions, and workshops available to members of all businesses, professions, and industries. Finding these is usually just a

---

5 You can access the SBA SCORE website at: https://www.sba.gov/local-assistance/resource-partners/score-business-mentoring

matter of staying connected to your networking systems and reading your trade journals. Often major industries will hold annual conventions attended by members from all over the United States and even abroad. These conventions display the latest developments in the industry and offer talks by prominent members and workshops conducted by experts in various aspects of the business.

Read, Read, Read: As I approach the close of this chapter, I want to loop back to the beginning. Dr. Ben Carson's wise mother discovered the power of reading and instilled it into young Ben, who began to read avidly and, in the process, turned his life around. Dr. Carson is not the only celebrity to recognize the power of reading. Earlier in the chapter, I listed several historical figures—such as Lincoln, Faraday, Edison, and Twain—whose primary education came through reading. It may surprise you to learn that, even today, some of the wealthiest and most successful people of our time attribute much of their success to the power of reading.

We often hear that money makes money. But these successful people would disagree. They know that knowledge makes money. In fact, someone has said that money is made of knowledge. Some of today's most successful entrepreneurs—such as Warren Buffet, Elon Musk, Bill Gates, Steve Jobs, Mark Zuckerberg, and Mark Cuban—have applied that principle to reach their spectacular goals. What do these people have in common? They read.

When asked how he learned to construct rockets and where he got all his ideas, Elon Musk replied, "I read books." He said that, in elementary school, he read almost ten hours a day. As a boy, he read through the entire *Encyclopedia Britannica*. Warren Buffet spends five hours a day reading papers, investment information, and books. Bill Gates' father reported that his son was such a voracious reader that he had to make a rule that young Bill could not bring a book to the dinner table. Gates still reads fifty books every year. Mark Cuban, the billionaire owner of the Dallas Mavericks, reads three hours every day. Mark Zuckerberg, another avid reader, adds an important dimension to the power of reading. He reads not only to learn and keep up with business, but also for sheer pleasure, simply to increase the quality of his life.[6] Popular singer and TV personality Kelly Clarkson is an avid reader who strongly encourages her fans and viewers to read.

Here are two happy facts about reading. The first is that it is very inexpensive—often even free (my favorite price). Used bookstores sell volumes for pennies on the dollar. Almost any book you might want is available free with a card from your public library. Most internet information costs nothing but the effort of swatting away continual pop-up ads.

The second happy fact about reading is that information on almost any possible subject you can imagine is instantly available to almost everyone. Are you as amazed as I am at the limitless variety of subjects accessible on the internet at the mere click of a mouse or swipe of a finger? We truly live within a big-bang explosion of information. Vast stores of relevant knowledge are waiting out there for you to tap into them to improve your business and your life exponentially.

Keep the Educational Wheels Turning

Take careful note of Mark Zuckerberg's philosophy as mentioned above. He reads not only for business knowledge but also to improve the quality of his life. Always remember that the real goal

---

6 Adapted from "Why All Billionaires Read Every Day – Billionaire Habits of Success," Youtube.com. https://www.youtube.com/watch?v=g0nJdJQbDEg Accessed November 1, 2023.

is excellence in life—not just in your vocation. Broaden your knowledge by learning in other useful areas such as art, music, religion, history, or literature. Don't settle for being one-dimensional. To live life to the fullest, you want to achieve excellence in broader, human areas such as family, church, and community relations. As I have said before and will say again and again before you finish this book, exponential excellence is achieved when your life exudes happiness, contentment, joy, freedom, and peace.

Eliminate Encumbrances

"I would like to travel light on this journey of life, to get rid of the encumbrances I acquire each day. . . . The most difficult thing to let go is myself, that self which, coddled and cozened, becomes smaller as it becomes heavier."

—author Madeleine L'Engle

In the movie *The Mission*, Rodrigo Mendoza (played by Robert DeNiro) is a ruthless Spanish slave trader in eighteenth-century South America. The man is brutal, heartless, and murderous. He lives by capturing natives and selling them as slaves to colonial plantations. When his captured slaves escape, he traps and kills them.

Mendoza learns that his fiancée is in love with his half-brother, and in a fit of rage he kills him in a duel. Though he is acquitted, he becomes despondent over the downward trajectory of his evil life.

While in this contrite condition, he is visited and converted by a missionary priest named Father Gabriel (Jeremy Irons).

As penance for his life of evil, Mendoza bundles up all his armor and weapons, ties the bundle to his body, and drags it about on the ground behind him wherever he goes. Compelled to face the native tribe he has wronged, he climbs the cliff to the top of the waterfall where the tribe lives with great effort, dragging the heavy weight behind him throughout the ascent.

He finally reaches the top, and as he drags the bundle toward the village, the natives see him approaching and come toward him with machetes in hand. Thinking this is the end, Mendoza resigns himself to his fate. He knows he deserves death for the horrors he has inflicted on these people. But instead of killing him, the natives use their machetes to cut away the burden he has been bearing and heave it over the cliff into the river below.

Through this stunning act of forgiveness, Mendoza, now rid of the encumbrance that has held him back, is free to live a new and productive life.

Encumbrances that Hold Us Back

Rodrigo Mendoza was heavily encumbered by the weight of the now-useless weapons of his evil past. That bundle, however, was merely the outward symbol of his real burden, which was the heavy guilt he could not release until those he had wronged lifted it from him. Like Mendoza, we too will never be free to pursue the life of joy, peace, happiness, freedom, and contentment we crave until we get rid of our own heavy encumbrances.

What encumbrances are weighing you down and holding you back from a life of excellence? You may be able to identify many, such as problems of the past, resentments, unresolved conflict, or fear of failure. But I will bet that most of them can be sorted under four main headings: enemies, ego, envy, and excuses. Let us look at each of these debilitating weights to show how they hold us back and how we can get rid of them.

The Encumbrance of Enemies

What enemies are keeping us from achieving our goals? "That's easy," every businessman may say. "Our enemies are our competitors. Walgreens' enemy is CVS. Pepsi's enemy is Coca-Cola. Ford's enemy is General Motors." Not so. Your competitors can actually help you. Competition prevents us from lapsing into complacency and spurs us to excellence. We work harder to provide a better product or service when we face competitors offering the same wares. Observing them carefully can teach us better practices or warn us of practices to avoid.

Your enemies may appear to be those on the opposite side of the political, moral, or identity spectrum who cannot tolerate your ideology. But as Arthur Brooks tells us, it is often possible to build bridges spanning these vast chasms. He relates the story of a huge Black Lives Matter (BLM) crowd arriving on the National Mall in Washington, D.C., to confront a massive Trump rally. A major and likely bloody confrontation seemed inevitable until the leader of the Trump rally invited the BLM leader onstage to speak to the Trump supporters. Given this graciously offered opportunity, the BLM leader chose to reciprocate in kind. Instead of shouting and responding with animosity, he chose to emphasize to find goals the two groups might find in common. Confrontation was averted. The two leaders became friends. This did not mean they agreed on basic beliefs, but they learned that each had reasons for his belief, and that they were both human beings pursuing personal aspirations despite their differences.[7]

---

7 Arthur C. Brooks, *Love Your Enemies* (New York: HarperCollins, 2019), 5–10.

This story illustrates the best way to get rid of enemies: Turn them into friends. Often even those who have radically diverse views can find enough commonality and humanity in each other to defuse the rising contempt that currently engulfs our world.

Your enemies may sometimes appear to be friends or even family members who try to discourage you from pursuing the path of excellence you have chosen. We are tempted to say, "With friends like these, who needs enemies?" We must remember that while these people cannot understand the passion that drives you, they are not your enemies. They have your best interest at heart and want you to achieve success. We would do well to listen to those who warn us that the field we have chosen is too glutted for success or will never pay much or lacks the prestige they think you should seek. But after all is said, remember that you still retain the power to choose your own avenue to excellence. As J. K. Rowling said, "It takes a great deal of bravery to stand up to our enemies, but just as much to stand up to our friends."

I am not trying to convey a Pollyanna attitude here. I realize that we all will encounter real opposition from people who dislike us or what we do and will attempt to undermine or cancel us. Anyone who accomplishes anything will inevitably face opposition. In a corporate environment, your enemy may be the person in the next office or cubicle—one who envies your successes and tries to undermine you behind your back, or the supervisor who tries to claim your achievements as his own. It is worthwhile to get rid of these encumbrances by the most peaceful means possible. But we must realize that sometimes, conciliation will remain beyond our reach. As Victor Hugo said, "You have enemies? Good. That means you've stood up for something, sometime in your life." Opposition is no excuse for failing to move forward.

The enemies I have trotted out so far are the easiest to overcome. But there is one enemy that is likely to give you real and constant trouble. This enemy was identified in Walt Kelly's classic comic strip *Pogo* when Pogo parodied Admiral Oliver Perry's famous quote by saying, "We have met the enemy, and he is us." That statement points to the person who can truly be your worst enemy. It could be you. As influential English Baptist preacher Charles Spurgeon put it, "Beware of no man more than of yourself; we carry our worst enemies within us."

Most of us carry within us the heavy burdens of self-doubt, negligence, lethargy, fear, failure, discouragement, and a legion of other weights that drag us down and undermine excellence. Often these enemies appear as subtle voices that insinuate debilitating attitudes in our heads, dissolving our courage to act. Those voices say, "You can't make an A in this class; settle for a C." "You'll never get that job; don't bother even to apply." "You can't write a book; don't waste your time trying."

That last voice is the one that has intruded into my thoughts many times while writing this book. Is what I am writing really any good, or am I a fool for thinking I might be the new Stephen R. Covey?

To get rid of these enemies, follow the advice of Polonius in Shakespeare's *Hamlet*: "Know yourself." Few of us dare to look deeply into our own souls to truly know ourselves—to discover the traits and attitudes hiding there that can undermine our best efforts. We are afraid of what we will find there. But to get rid of those enemies inside, you must force yourself to do a regular self-assessment to root out the unwanted demons (are there wanted demons?) that undermine your pursuit of excellence. I know it is hard to be honest about our own faults. We cover them up so much that we fool even ourselves into thinking they are not there. And when we fool ourselves, we make fools of ourselves.

An old Cherokee told his grandson, "My son, there is a battle between two wolves inside us all. One is Evil. It is anger, jealousy, greed, resentment, inferiority, lies, and ego. The other is Good. It is joy, peace, love, hope, humility, kindness, empathy, and truth." The boy pondered for a while, and then asked, "Grandfather, which wolf wins?" The old man quietly replied, "The one you feed."

To ensure a realistic self-assessment, get a friend who knows you well to help you see what you tend to hide from yourself—the wolf inside which you feed the most. Force to the surface those faults that hold you back from excellence. Once they are exposed to the light, it is much easier to cut them away and heave them into the river.

The Encumbrance of Ego

Egotism is like glaucoma; it's an "I" problem. It distorts one's focus on reality. It magnifies his imagined strengths and blocks his vision of his weaknesses. Ego affects every human on earth.

Ego inflation is closely connected with pride. Theologians tell us that pride is the chief of the seven deadly sins. In today's usage, however, the word pride has both a good meaning and a bad one. If I say I'm proud of the company I built, I can mean one of two things: I may mean I am gratified by the fact that I was able to apply my talents and abilities in a positive way that accomplished a benefit to humanity. Nothing wrong with that. But on the other hand, I may mean "Man, people will now see me as a big-time entrepreneur who has built something that very few people have my skills and talent to accomplish." Pride in the first sense focuses on the positive nature of the result. Pride in the second sense focuses on me and how I want to appear superior in the eyes of others. It is motivated by ego, which feeds on honors and recognition like a glutton feeds on pizza and burgers. Pride in the good sense is validated simply by accomplishing the task at hand, even if no honor or recognition follows.

C. S. Lewis points out that it is proper for a general to be gratified with victory. In victory he fulfilled his duty and protected his country. Victory is the proper reward for a general. But if the victorious general glories not in his selfless fulfillment of duty but rather in the hero worship he has gained—the articles in the paper, the accolades of leaders, the medals and promotions he receives— he has stepped away from legitimate pride into self-centered pride, which is the work of the inflated ego.

I really hate to have to tell you this, but you too are plagued by this second form of pride. You too have an ego that wants to achieve status in the eyes of others by magnifying your accomplishments and covering up your failures. Oh, yes you do! And the sooner you admit it, the better. So quit arguing with me and read on. I'm not picking on you, because a prideful ego is a problem every person born on Earth faces. Though I have found that some people believe ego to be a positive motivating factor, experience and observation show clearly that the opposite is true. Ego is an impediment to excelling exponentially. When you spot these people, you tend to run the other way.

Ego gets in the way. It distorts the truth. It inhibits growth because it makes you think you already have everything it takes to be a winner and thus prevents you from taking needed steps to correct flaws and improve your knowledge and skills. If I already think I am superior, why bother to improve? To become infatuated with our own talents and accomplishments is the mark of a narcissist, and it is something we all detest when we see it in others.

What damage does ego inflation do to us? First, it damages our most cherished and important relationships. It almost cost me my future wife. Three years after my high school graduation, I attended a young adult dance at a church. After dancing for a while, I spotted a beautiful woman and asked her to dance with me. She introduced herself as Lanelle and said she recognized me from high school. While we were slow dancing, she clutched the back of my shirt and said, "Boy, you are hot." I couldn't resist a comment like that, so I replied, "Yeah, that's what all the girls tell me." I meant it for humor, but she took it as an expression of a massive ego. She didn't want to see me again. (I can not leave the story hanging there. I continued to pursue Lanelle, and now she and I have been married for 34 years and counting.)

No one enjoys being around a person with a massive ego. His focus on himself overshadows his concern for others. He is the only important person in his life, and others are shunted to the margins. Ego comes between us and our families and friends. It can drive away customers and clients. Even the adoring fans of sports figures tend to drop away when their hero's ego is revealed in his comments and speeches. In his book, *Ego is the Enemy*, Ryan Holiday wrote, "A critic of Napoleon nailed it when remarking: 'He [Napoleon] despises the nation whose applause he seeks.' He couldn't help but see the French people as pieces to be manipulated, people he had to be better than, people who, unless they were totally, unconditionally supportive of him, were against him."[8]

The trick is to learn to see the tendency toward ego inflation in ourselves. To rise to this difficult level of objectivity, we must learn to get outside ourselves—to develop a kind of detachment that allows us to see ourselves as others see us. This is difficult because no one is objective when it comes to self-assessment. We all have blind spots. As I advised in the above section, the solution is to have a

8 Ryan Holiday, *Ego is the Enemy* (Edmonton, Alberta: Portfolio Publishing, 2016).

close friend give you the real truth about yourself. Tell him or her that you want this truth, even if it is hideously ugly. And when you receive that truth, you must resist the impulse to be shocked, offended, defensive, or to start spouting excuses. And to restrain your impulse to knock him across the room. If you feel offended when your friend tries to correct you or tells you the truth about yourself, that very feeling of offense is an indication of your ego problem. Objective self-awareness that you have the problem is the first step to overcoming it.

The ego fights to survive. We enjoy magnifying ourselves even though the bigger the ego, the less self we have to magnify. Often ego is a cover-up for insecurity. As we noted in the section on enemies, we feel inadequate in our central selves, so we focus on our possessions, work, social status, knowledge, physical appearance, special abilities, family history, belief systems, or other identifications that we deem superior. The problem is that none of these things is really you. The real you is the self that exists beneath all these accumulated possessions and characteristics.

Above, I noted that feeling offended can be a hint that you are ego-driven. Feeling offended, responding in anger, or displaying hurt feelings are all defenses against criticism, and an inflated ego cannot stand criticism. We want others to see us as we see ourselves, and we tend to see ourselves through rose-tinted glasses. Our ego constantly attempts to pass out those glasses to others so they will see us as being as magnificent as we think we are.

David A. Bednar, former president of Brigham Young University–Idaho, gives us even deeper reasons why we should not be offended:

> When we believe or say we have been offended, we usually
> mean we feel insulted, mistreated, snubbed, or disrespect-

ed. And certainly clumsy, embarrassing, unprincipled, and mean-spirited things do occur in our interactions with other people that would allow us to take offense. However, it ultimately is impossible for another person to offend you or to offend me. Indeed, believing that another person offended us is fundamentally false. To be offended is a *choice* we make; it is not a *condition* inflicted or imposed upon us by someone or something else.[9]

In his book, *Unoffendable*, Brant Hansen wrote, "We should forfeit our right to be offended. That means forfeiting our right to hold on to anger. When we do this, we will be making a sacrifice that is very pleasing to God. It strikes at our very pride. It forces us not only to think about humility, but to actually be humble... Forfeiting our right to anger makes us deny ourselves and makes us others centered. When we start living this way, it changes everything."[10]

The Encumbrance of Envy

The 1984 film *Amadeus* portrays the eighteenth-century composer Antonio Salieri as being bitterly envious of Mozart's spectacular natural ability and success. While in real life, Mozart and Salieri were described as contemporaries with great respect for each other, the film took creative liberties. According to the film, Salieri was a highly religious, dedicated man who deeply resented the fact that Mozart, with his crass manners and profligate bohemian lifestyle, could whip out genius-level operas that far outstripped Salieri's best efforts. Salieri's extreme envy drove him to bring about the death of Mozart in hopes of claiming his final masterpiece as his own. The

---

9 David A. Bednar, "And Nothing Shall Offend Them," *Liahona Magazine*, October 2006, 90.

10 Brant Hansen, *Unoffendable* (Nashville, TN: Thomas Nelson, 2023).

film goes on to show that guilt over what he had done drove Salieri to insanity. Although historians today do not believe that Salieri killed Mozart, the film shows vividly the destructive effects of envy.

Aristotle defined envy as "the pain caused by the good fortune of others."[11] Kant defined it as "a reluctance to see our own well-being overshadowed by another's because the standard we use to see how well off we are is not the intrinsic worth of our own well-being but how it compares with that of others."[12]

To envy means to feel resentful because another person possesses something we want but do not have or has achieved something we want to achieve or failed to achieve. One might envy another's beauty or wealth or a coworker's promotion.

Some psychologists divide envy into two categories: malicious and benign. Malicious envy wants to bring the rival down at all costs. The envy of Salieri in the movie was malicious. He was determined to destroy the man he envied. Benign envy, on the other hand, spurs the envious person to work to get what he desires. But the emotion that pushes him to succeed is not a positive one. He strives to get what he wants in order to outdo his rival rather than in a quest for personal excellence. So envy in both forms—malicious and benign— are negative feelings that make one unhappy. They torment us with a sense of unease and emptiness gnawing at our insides. In both cases, envy puts the focus on comparison with another person rather than evaluating oneself by an objective standard. This tendency to compare ourselves with others points out one thing we must remember about envy in either form: Envy only hurts you, not the person you

---

11 Aristotle, "Rhetoric," Wikipedia, https://en.wikipedia.org/wiki/Rhetoric_(Aristotle), accessed September 27, 2023.

12 Immanuel Kant: *Metaphysics and Morals*, Wikipedia, https://en.wikipedia.org/wiki/Metaphysics_of_Morals, accessed September 27, 2023.

are envious of. Most likely the other person does not know you are envious of him or her.

No one wants to be envious, but envy can catch us by surprise and rise up unexpectedly when we encounter some quality or accomplishment in another person that we desire to have for ourselves. The antidote to envy is to realize that it is merely a feeling; it is not based on reality. The reality is that we, as individuals with our own unique set of qualities and abilities, are not supposed to have all the skills, achievements, or innate qualities as everyone else. As I have pointed out elsewhere in this book, it is necessary for all of us to have widely differing qualities and abilities in order to create and sustain a functioning society.

Recognizing this need for different aptitudes and qualities rather than craving those which we do not have is the first step in overcoming envy. It is a step toward contentment—being content with what we have and content to be who we are rather than allowing envy to make us want to be like someone else. I am reminded of something the actor Bruce Lee said: "Always be yourself—express yourself, have faith in yourself. Do not go out and look for a successful personality and duplicate it." Comparing ourselves with others is always a downer. We were not meant to be clones or assembly line robots. Each of us is utterly unique—which is to say, we are extraordinary—and the key to happiness and contentment is to find our own qualities that give us aptitudes to accomplish the goals that we were designed to accomplish. This is the real key to peace with oneself and the way to be content with what one has. It is the way to banish envy.

The Encumbrance of Excuses

Benjamin Franklin said, "He that is good for making excuses is seldom good for anything else." Another Ben, Dr. Ben Carson, put it like this: "People who fail in life are people who find lots of excuses." Both statements are true. The day you stop making excuses for your failures will be the day you take full responsibility for yourself and your actions. That will be the day when you begin to excel exponentially.

The person who takes full responsibility for his actions exhibits nobility, courage, and a high sense of personal responsibility. He exhibits nobility in that he doesn't lay blame for his failures on other people, on circumstances, or on unexpected problems. He takes on the task and bears the result, good or bad. He sees himself as an agent capable of making a difference, and thus he knows that success or failure rests on his own shoulders. When a woman asked her friend how she was doing, the friend replied, "I guess I'm doing okay under the circumstances." The woman responded, "Well, what are you doing under there?" People who take responsibility for their actions do not camp "under the circumstances." They get on top of them. They are not victims of circumstances, but masters of them. That is nobility.

The responsible person exhibits courage in that he ventures out to undertake a difficult task, realizing that failure is possible. Though he hopes for success and expects it, if failure happens, he can bear it with his head up. But he cannot bear the stigma of being a person who did not try simply because the task was difficult.

The responsible person exhibits personal responsibility in that he avoids today's common victim mentality that lays the cause of failure at the feet of everything or everyone but himself. In our day, social expectations and peer pressure are common influences on our goals and actions. And when we fail, they become classic excuses that many fall back on to justify their failure.

Many people excuse their failure to move forward on their past failures. "I failed at this before, so what's the use in trying again." But those who are committed to excellence hang in there and try again. Mega-bestselling author Stephen King accumulated thirty rejections before a publisher finally accepted his first novel. Walt Disney was fired from the *Kansas City Star* newspaper because he "lacked imagination and had no good ideas." His first animated cartoon company went bankrupt.

Robert the Bruce was defeated six times in battles against England's King Edward II for Scotland's independence. In retreat and hiding one night in an abandoned barn, the discouraged warrior was ready to give up until he watched a spider building a web across a wide expanse of rafters. The spider tried six times but failed to make the span. But she succeeded on the seventh. Inspired by the persistent little arachnid, Bruce fought a seventh battle that defeated the English and won Scottish independence.

These men did not use their past failures as excuses. They regrouped, held to their vision, and kept striving for excellence.

I often hear of people blaming their failures on their upbringing or childhood abuse. Country music icon Shania Twain talks of being raised in poverty and suffered severe sexual, emotional, and psychological abuse from her stepfather. When her mother and stepfather were killed in a car accident, Shania raised her young siblings in extreme poverty. Yet she did not let these early traumas keep her from becoming one of America's most successful country singers whose recordings have sold multiple millions.

Bottom line: excuses seldom excuse. What happened in the past—failures, abuse, defeats, rejection—are never reasons to give up and not try to achieve your dream. If the dream becomes truly impossible, as it would seem if you are a singer who loses her hearing or a pitcher who loses an arm, that still is no excuse to drop out of the race for excellence. It simply means you choose an alternate dream and keep going. Joy, peace, happiness, freedom, and contentment are always possible, even for the severely handicapped. Just ask Helen Keller.

Enemies, egos, envy, and excuses: We've all got to deal with these pesky obstacles, but none of them is an adequate reason to deter us from our goal. Love your enemies, let go of your ego, eliminate your envy, and put excuses out of your reach. These four encumbrances will block your path to joy, happiness, freedom, peace, or contentment. If you don't let them distract you from your focus on your vision, you'll greatly increase your chances of excelling exponentially.

Exercise Your Essential Endowments

"No one can become fully aware of the very essence of another human being unless he loves him."

—Viktor E. Frankl

The great pianist Arthur Rubenstein was walking down a New York street when a young man with a map in his hand, obviously lost, stopped him and said, "Mister, could you tell me how I can get to Carnegie Hall?" Rubenstein looked him in the eye and said, "Practice, practice, practice."

I do not know whether that story is true, whether the great pianist misunderstood the question, or whether he deliberately used it to make a larger point. But I *do* know that the point he made is a good one. No matter what your talent is, no matter how valuable the assets you are endowed with, they will never get you to a life of excellence unless you exercise them diligently, intentionally, vigorously, and regularly. That means practice, practice, practice.

A true example of the power of focused exercise is that of Wilma Rudolph. Born in 1940, she was the twentieth of twenty-two children in a poor, black family in Tennessee. Shortly after she learned to walk, she contracted polio. Doctors said she would never walk again.

At age six, Wilma was fitted with leg braces, enabling her to hobble awkwardly. Encouraged by her family, she worked diligently at her physical therapy, and by age eight, she could walk without braces. She continued to exercise until she not only walked normally but also began to run. Soon, she was outrunning other girls. In high school, she became a basketball star and excelled in track and field events.

After graduation, Wilma Rudolph enrolled in Tennessee State University. She made the track team and came in third in the 100- and 200-meter races at the 1959 Pan American Games. Then came her crowning achievement. She won a spot on the 1960 U.S. Olympic team. At the games in Rome, she won gold in the 100-meter race, the 200-meter race, and the 4x100-meter relay, becoming the first woman to win three gold medals in one Olympics. She set an Olympic record in the opening heat of the 200-meter race, for which she was often called "the fastest woman in the world."[13]

Wilma Rudolph's story shows how one can achieve greatness through diligent exercise and effort. This principle applies not only to overcoming obstacles, as Wilma did, but also to making the best use of the normal abilities and talents we all possess. These elemental, inborn assets that we all share are what I call endowments because

13 "Wilma Rudolph, African-American Olympic Legend," on the website *Black History in America* (myblackhistory.net) http://www.myblackhistory.net/Wilma_Rudolph.htm, Accessed April 26, 2023.

God has endowed each of us with them as tools for living rich and full lives in our daily functions. When any one of these endowments is dysfunctional, our lives become impaired, and we cannot achieve the excellence we desire. There are many areas of endowment that we could address, but I have selected four elemental ones as my focus in this chapter. They are the physical, mental, spiritual, and social. Let us explore these God-given endowments one by one and learn how exercising them can help us to achieve excellence.

Exercising Our Physical Endowment

The apostle Paul wrote, "...bodily exercise profits a little, but godliness is profitable for all things..." (1 Timothy 4:8 NKJV). I suspect some people read this passage with a sigh of relief, thinking it tells us that physical exercise is of minimal value, so we should focus on spiritual things. But Paul flips the coin in 1 Corinthians 6:19 (KJV) where he urges us to take care in how we use the body because "your body is the temple of the Holy Ghost which is in you." Your body is one of your key endowments that must be cared for and kept pure.

The body is critically important because it is the house you live in. It is where your other endowments—mental, spiritual, and social—reside. The health of your body affects your brain, the seat of your mental health. It affects your spiritual health because, without a body, you cannot perform the spiritual duties of feeding the hungry, helping the needy, or ministering to the sick. Without a healthy body, your social life also deteriorates, isolating you from others and impairing communication.

The most obvious (and least popular) way of caring for your body is to get sufficient exercise. (If you got a dollar every time you heard that, you would probably be wealthy by now.) How much and what kind of exercise you need depends on your age and your goals. If you are twenty-five and a professional firefighter, you may need to spend frequent time working out in a gym or fitness center. Not all of us, however, feel a need for six-pack abs, pumped-up pecs, or beefy biceps. Even so, we all need regular exercise of some kind to keep our bodies fit and functioning.

The key is to maintain self-discipline to exercise regularly. My doctor told me to exercise regularly, so I make it a point to do it once a year. Joking aside, I do exercise regularly so that I am doing what I tell others they should be doing. We live in an age of distractions and entertainments. Television morphs us into couch potatoes. We stare at electronic devices for hours as our dinner turns to fat and expands our waistlines. Sitting for hours compresses our leg veins, impairing blood flow. Our muscles lose tone and strength. Our bodies will turn into jelly-like blobs if we do not muster up the will to exercise regularly.

While on the topic of caring for the body, I will briefly mention five other items critical to your physical health. The five items are 1) get plenty of sleep, 2) eat a balanced diet, 3) slacken your frenetic pace, 4) drink plenty of water, and 5) listen to your body. But after all that is said and done, I am still going to circle back around and harp again on the need for exercise. The most important thing is to do something to get your body moving—and I do not mean just from the couch to the refrigerator!

Exercising Your Mental Endowment

Just as a neglected body gets flabby and dysfunctional without proper exercise and care, so does the mind. It is easy to allow negativity, worry, anxiety, resentment, stress, or other destructive mental behaviors to leave us with couch-potato minds.

According to psychotherapist Dr. Barton Goldsmith, all the knowledge and experience we gather about life is rendered useless by a negative attitude. The more we feed negativity, the stronger it gets. Negative attitudes usually grow out of painful or oppressive experiences. Ruminating on these experiences, even if our goal is to figure out where we went wrong, can become a mental prison. The key, Dr. Goldsmith says, "is to break out of this mental space and into a place where you can relax your emotional being."[14]

The solution is to monitor your thinking. When you catch those negative thoughts clouding your mind, shine a light on them. Catch them in the headlights and see them for what they are. This exercise may not produce an immediate turnaround, but simple awareness of what is going on to cloud your mind means a fix is in progress.

As exercises to change negative thinking, Dr. Goldsmith recommends reading, writing, playing music, and cleaning or organizing. Other psychologists expand the list to include going for a walk, taking a shower, setting a small goal, journal writing, taking up a sport or hobby, and spending time with a positive person. These are mind-altering techniques that tend to cleanse your mind of the negativity that blocks your path to excellence.

I have found that reading positive books, articles, and literature, playing board games such as Scrabble or Boggle, or playing online mind games such as Dictionary.com or similar word games, puzzle games, or trivia quizzes can sharpen one's mental health.

Here are some additional exercises for improving your mental health.

---

14 Barton Goldsmith, "Managing Your Mind," psychologytoday.com, November 6, 2019, https://www.psychologytoday.com/us/blog/emotional-fitness/201911/managing-your-mind

Take Time to Relax and Recharge. Many hard-charging business professionals shun downtime because they fear it diminishes productivity. The opposite is true. Relaxing, shifting focus to pleasurable activities or entertainment can unclench the fist our mind has become, recharge our mental batteries, and increase focus, creativity, and energy, making us more productive and efficient. Stephen Covey calls it "sharpen the saw."

Stop Multitasking. Multitasking is touted as a positive ability, but it does more harm than good. It is a leading cause of brain fog and scrambled thinking. Learning to focus on one thing at a time produces a clearer mind and leads to greater efficiency.

Banish Worry. We are all guilty of worry even though we know it does not help a whit. What is worry? It is a persistent, unrelenting focus on problems or dangers over which we have no control. Of course, we can also focus on problems or dangers over which we *do* have control. This differs from worry because its purpose is to find a solution. It is not a worry to spend a lot of focus on how you are going to arrange your finances to pay for your daughter's college education. It *is a worry* to spend a lot of time obsessed about whether she will study or party.

I like this advice from Joyce Meyer: "When you begin to worry, go find something to do. Get busy being a blessing to someone; do something fruitful. Talking about your problem or sitting alone, thinking about it, does no good; it serves only to make you miserable. Above all else, remember that worrying is totally useless. Worrying will not solve your problem."[15]

Focus on the Positive. By exercising control over what we think about when our minds are free, we create our own mental environ-

15 Joyce Meyer, brainyquote.com, https://www.brainyquote.com/authors/joyce-meyer-quotes Accessed April 27, 2023.

ment. Our minds need positive direction. If we allow them to drift, they naturally float downstream. What we have often heard is true: An idle mind is the devil's workshop. I have adopted the following scripture as a personal habit because it offers an excellent solution to mental contamination: "Whatsoever things are true, whatsoever things are honest, whatsoever things are just, whatsoever things are pure, whatsoever things are lovely, whatsoever things are of good report; if there be any virtue, and if there be any praise, think on these things" (Philippians 4:8 KJV). By directing our thoughts toward the true, the beautiful, the positive, the creative, the pure, and the virtuous, we furnish our mind with values that let in light and dispel darkness. This light brightens our attitudes, our outlook, our creativity, our optimism, and increases our joy.

Seek help when needed. No one stands alone. We all sometimes need the help of others to maintain our mental fitness and avoid damaging negativity. Often when you are wrestling with a dilemma for which you see no solution, it is good to have a friend or family member to whom you can lay out the problem to be seen through a fresh set of eyes.

If feelings of negativity or depression begin to creep into your mind, seek the help of a friend who understands and can ease you back into a positive outlook. If your problem runs deeper, as in clinical depression or debilitating anxiety, do not hesitate to seek professional help from qualified experts. As my mental health counselor son Zack says, "There is no shame in seeking professional help at any stage of difficulty. Seeking help early can often redirect your path before it leads to much worse mental health problems. Whether it's preventative, early in the process, or severe, all efforts to improve mental health are a worthy endeavor. We excel more when we find physical, emotional, and mental peace and strength."[16]

---

16 Zackary Butterfield, CMHC.

Exercising Your Spiritual Endowment

We achieve spiritual wellness by aligning ourselves with guiding beliefs and principles that give direction to our lives. Following these beliefs and principles gives us a sense of meaning and purpose. By aligning ourselves with an overarching belief, our inner being experiences harmony with unseen realities.

I think most of us recognize the presence within ourselves of an invisible entity that we call our spirit. There are varied beliefs about the spirit, and I think most non-religious people view what we call the spirit as the central self, our deepest essence. Despite these varied beliefs, most people seem to recognize that there is an endowment within us separate from the mind and body which affects our functioning and well-being as humans. With that in mind, let me suggest five exercises that will enhance your spiritual endowment.

Engage in regular prayer and meditation. Many people establish a regular habit of spending a specified part of their day in what they call "quiet time." This is usually fifteen to thirty minutes spent in reading their scriptures, meditating on what they read, and praying to God. This regimen puts the human spirit in contact with the divine Spirit and, over time, transforms your life by bringing it into greater alignment with deity.

Attend worship services. The major religions most prevalent in our nation encourage attendance to services or rituals in their churches, synagogues, temples, or other places of worship. These gatherings rejuvenate the spirit through teaching, communion with deity, and fellowship with fellow believers. The importance of this social contact with fellow believers can hardly be overemphasized. Connection with those who believe as we do reinforces our own commitment to those beliefs as well as our loyalty to those who share that commitment.

These worship and fellowship exercises create bonds with other believers and with deity, both of which enhance our spiritual well-being.

Spend time in nature. If you are like me, lying on a quilt spread on my backyard lawn and gazing up into deep, star-studded space gives me a sense of awe and wonder. It lifts my spirit and makes me realize I am part of something grand and beautiful, planned and created by the hand of a super-intelligent, super-powerful, super-artistic, and super-loving being.

Gazing into deep space is not the only source of these revelations. Many experience a connection with deity in the mountains, at the seashore, in the glory of spring blossoms, fall leaves, the songs of birds, a glowing sunset, or the endless variety of animal life. All nature bears the signature of the artist who made it, and connecting with nature lifts our spirits by enabling us to see ourselves as integral parts of his universal masterpiece.

Find and follow your purpose. To give meaning to our lives, we all need to feel that we are here for a reason. Most believers in God are convinced that he has endowed us with a created purpose, and finding and developing that purpose will give us the meaning we desire. Clues to finding that purpose can be many and varied. Your strongest interests can point the way. If mechanical things fascinate you, you may find your purpose in engineering. If it is words and reading, perhaps you should pursue writing. If you love to make things, you may be a potential architect, craftsman, or clothing designer. Or some human or societal need may arouse your sympathy and draw you into a service career involving caregiving, medicine, or social work.

Usually these clues will point the way to your purpose. Following them to find your field of activity and getting the right training to give you proficiency in them will help to expand your spiritual endowment and find meaning in your life.

Express gratitude. Have you ever taken the time to list the things in your life that you are grateful for? For Thanksgiving one year, my mother-in-law gave us a gratitude journal. She challenged us to write down the things we are grateful for over a thirty-day period. She made the following two stipulations: First, record three things per day. Second, do not duplicate any of the things you are grateful for. It was an enthralling experience. I now challenge you to do it. You can list not only possessions—such as your house, transportation, comforts, etc.—but also the people who brighten your life or influence you positively. Then include things like health, abilities, love, confidence, religion, environment—the list can go on and on. Gratitude tends to lift the spirit and generate a sense of well-being by focusing on the positive elements of your life.

Meet the needs of others. No matter what your career or profession, we all have an obligation to help our fellow strugglers. Human needs are all around us. Poverty, loss, sickness, grief, injury, and other disasters can happen to any of us. We are all dependent on each other, and those of us who are strong, healthy, well-off, and intact must be alert to opportunities to aid those who have, as Shakespeare put it, "suffered the slings and arrows of outrageous fortune." Our spiritual vitality depends on our willingness to meet the needs of the less fortunate.

Dispel guilt by seeking forgiveness. We have all felt guilt, so we all know what it is. It is the heavy weight we feel in our spirits when we have done something we know to be wrong. Guilt can be especially devastating when that wrong has hurt another person. Guilt is a debilitating downer. It can get a grip on one's life that completely chokes off peace and joy. So naturally, when we incur guilt by our wrong actions, we desperately seek ways to get rid of it.

Curious, I went to the internet to see what techniques counselors and psychologists advise for overcoming guilt. I was amazed at the variety of recommendations. Here's a sampling: Eliminate negative self-talk; realize it is okay to have needs; establish boundaries; realize that nobody's perfect; practice positive affirmations; learn from your mistakes; look for distractions; practice self-compassion.

Wow! The lists seemed to include everything but the one thing that will really work, and that is to seek forgiveness. This means going to the person you have wronged, admitting you were wrong, and asking forgiveness. Do not make the mistake of trying to excuse your deed. ("I wouldn't have done it, but you see, I was in a hurry." "I just wasn't feeling up to par that day.") And do not use the all-too common "if" apology: "I'm sorry *if* what I said hurt you." Such an apology implies that the offense was really on the part of the other person. She shouldn't have been so sensitive as to be hurt by what you said. The only valid apology is to say, "I am truly sorry for what I did. There was no excuse for such behavior. I don't deserve to be forgiven, but I dearly hope you can find it in your heart to forgive me." If possible, make amends for what you did. If it is something that cannot be undone, the need for forgiveness is all the more imperative.

Live by your principles. Perhaps the most common criticism of religious people is that they are all hypocrites. They do not live by what they believe. There is considerable basis for such criticism when we read reports of famous preachers or priests committing sexual sins. Or when our neighbors or coworkers see us overcharging customers, undercutting competitors, or violating contracts.

When our principles are true and we do our best to live by them, we align ourselves with reality. We feel inner peace because we are in harmony with the power that permeates the universe. A life in harmony with God exudes calmness, assurance, and a sense of inner well-being that enhances every area of life and propels it toward excellence.

Exercising Your Social Endowment

You cannot achieve excellence without exercising your social endowment. By social endowment, I refer to our need for association with other people, which involves the ability to relate well to them. Your social environment includes your family, friends, coworkers, competitors, and even strangers and opponents.

"No man is an island," said John Donne. No one is self-sufficient. We are all dependent on others for our well-being. Our interactions with others help to build a sense of belonging and self-worth. They provide opportunities to share our experiences, feelings, and ideas. Our closest social connections provide emotional support and allow us to support others.

With these benefits in mind, let us review several ways of exercising our social skills that can propel us toward a life of excellence.

Stay connected with other people. Regular relationships are critical to our social well-being. "Duh!" you say. "Isn't that too obvious to mention?" That may have been true in the past, but in this era of ubiquitous social media, electronic communication devices, and the growing number of employees now working offsite at home computers, it is easy to slip into habitual isolation and neglect the essential human need to socialize.

My self-employed friend, Myron, has offices in his home. He deals with his clients almost solely by email. He and his wife maintained an active social life that included visiting their daughters, eating out with friends, attending church events, hosting movie nights with friends or family, and traveling occasionally to visit friends in other cities. But when his wife died, it was easy for Myron to just stay at home, bury himself with work, and not muster up the energy to get up and get out. He sometimes went a whole day without saying a word. What woke him up to the depth of his isolation was when the phone rang one afternoon, and his voice was so raspy he had to clear his throat several times even to say "Hello." He realized he could easily become reclusive if he didn't take action. So, he began to involve himself deeper in church activities. He revived "dinner-and-movie" nights with his best friend and his wife. He increased his involvement with his daughters and grandchildren. And (this may sound crazy) he deliberately began to sing and talk to himself around the house just to keep his voice in shape and maintain his ability to converse.

Most of us already have a social network of family, friends, and coworkers to interact with, but as we go through life, we continually encounter new acquaintances with the potential of becoming part of our social circle. While we never want to reject anyone or write them off as a person deserving human respect, we must realize we cannot be real friends with just anyone and everyone. For this reason, it is important to cultivate healthy relationships—to be selective in who we invite into our closest circles. We have all encountered people whose anger or criticism darkened our mood. We have been trapped by chatterers who dominated the conversation or focused on running down other people. Sometimes patience requires that we endure such conversations. Still, for our own social well-being, we want to cultivate friendships with those who share our interests, outlook, values, and morality. We can engage in mutually beneficial exchanges that will build both parties up instead of undermining our emotional well-being.

Here are three suggestions for maintaining good relationships with those closest to you.

1. *Exercise effective communication skills.* I do not mean you need to become an orator or memorize a university grammar textbook. But if you want to maintain good relationships, your social skills must include the ability to communicate clearly and without causing "Hallmark moments." What are Hallmark moments? Let me explain:

    Hallmark movies (I became an expert on these movies while watching them with my wife during the COVID-19 pandemic) are commendable for offering generally clean and moral stories. But every storyline follows a repetitive formula. Toward the end of the movie, the couple who seem to be progressing toward marriage have a major falling out over a misunderstanding that severs the relationship. To make matters worse, the offended person refuses to listen to an explanation that would clear everything up and restore the relationship. These are what I call Hallmark moments—misunderstandings that provoke anger, hurt feelings, or offense—communication failures that can inadvertently break up friendships, business relationships, romances, and even family bonds.

    Avoiding Hallmark moments is the responsibility of both the speaker and the hearer. The speaker must take care to be clear and direct, and the hearer must request clarification if he or she questions any part of what the speaker said. The speaker may have stated the case poorly, or the hearer may have assumed a meaning not intended. Rather than respond with anger or offense, exchanging a few more questions would enable both parties to know exactly what was meant.

2. *Listen more than you talk.* As someone said, "If you think communication is all about talking, you haven't been listening." Listening is an often-overlooked element in good communication. Good listening skills involve more than the ear. There is a bit of acting involved, which means you need to pay attention to your body language and maintain eye contact with whoever is speaking. It helps to nod in agreement now and then when the speaker makes a significant point.

   Listening can test your patience if you are caught by a talker who does not know when to stop and does not pause to give you a chance to respond or even to politely excuse yourself from further listening. While interrupting is generally a no-no, at times even the most patient listener may find it necessary. Developing these good listening skills will greatly improve your social excellence. And, while we are talking about conversational acuity, let us put the shoe on the other foot. It is also a good thing to develop succinct talking skills so your listener will not feel the need to interrupt you for prattling on too long. My good friend, Tony, has mastered this skill. He always ends his thoughts or stories by saying, "the end," as if to say, "I'm done. You can respond now."

3. *Get control of social media.* It is a paradox of our time that smartphones and social media, which were developed as aids to more effective social interaction, have instead increased human isolation to the point of alarm. Smartphones and social media tend to draw people away from direct contact with each other and into the impersonal sphere of the internet. How often have you seen people sitting on the four sides of a restaurant table, all staring silently at their phone screens without a word passing between them?

Social media outlets were designed to facilitate social interaction. But they often become wastebaskets for inane and meaningless posts about uninteresting trivial matters or arenas of angry and vitriolic conflict. Yet many people are now addicted to social media. Recent studies have revealed that young people now prefer to communicate by texting or social media rather than face-to-face in person. It is clear if we are to keep our social endowment healthy, we must get control of our social media usage. Or, like a recovering alcoholic, swear off it altogether. (I will have more to say about social media in Chapter 7.)

Exercising the four universal human endowments addressed in this chapter will help you not only to become more efficient in your endeavors and pursuits, but I am also convinced they will help you become a better and happier person. This means you achieve not only excellence in doing, but also excellence in being.

Emulate Good Examples

"I'd rather see a sermon than hear one any day;
I'd rather one should walk with me than merely tell the way.
The eye's a better pupil and more willing than the ear,
Fine counsel is confusing, but example's always clear."
—Edgar A. Guest

ark Twain famously said, "Few things are harder to put up with than the annoyance of a good example." Obviously, Mr. Twain had his witty tongue firmly planted in his cheek. What the quote does show us, however, (though in a backhanded way), is the *power* of a good example. It wouldn't be annoying if it did not inspire. Someone's good example obviously moved the reluctant Twain to get off his duff and take action he knew he should take but lacked the desire to do it. To achieve excellence, it helps to seek out good examples that inspire us to action and draw from them principles that will spur us toward our goals.

The power of good examples explains why we have heroes. The value of our heroes, whether in books, movies, or real life, is that when we see them doing great things, we are inspired to do great things. Especially if their greatness grows out of trying circumstances such as poverty, prejudice, or handicaps. Their example inspires us to say, "If he can do it, I can do it." "If she could overcome her debilitating fear, I can overcome mine." "If he could grasp that unreachable star, then so can I."

One of the most inspiring stories that demonstrates the power of an example is that of the British track runner Roger Bannister. When Bannister began his career in 1946, runners had long aspired to run the mile in less than four minutes. At that time, it had never been done, and many experts thought the four-minute mile to be physically unachievable. When Bannister began running, his fellow Englishman, Sydney Wooderson, held the world record for running the mile at 4 minutes and 4.2 seconds.

Bannister's first mile run was recorded at a relatively slow 4:13. He increased his training and began to bring his numbers down until he reached 4.07.8 in a prominent 1950 British competition. But over the next two years, he suffered several defeats, even failing to win a medal in the 1952 Olympics.

Spurred on by his failure, Bannister seriously intensified his training regimen. In May 1953, he bested Wooderson's record by running the mile in 4:03.6. This made him realize the four-minute mile was not out of reach. Then, on May 6, 1954, Roger Bannister ran the mile against five competitors in a meet at the University of Oxford viewed by 3,000 spectators. He crossed the finish line at 3 minutes, 59.4 seconds, the first man in recorded history to run the mile in under 4 minutes. When his record was announced, the crowd went wild.

Here is why I kicked off this chapter about emulating examples with Roger Bannister's story. Shortly after he broke the 4-minute barrier, runners all over the world began to run the mile in under 4 minutes. In fact, his record lasted only forty-six days when it was broken by Finland's John Lundy at 3:58 minutes. Since that time, the record has continued to come down and has been held since 1999 by Hicham El Guerrouj of Morocco at a time of 3:43.13. My point is this: Examples show us that the "impossible" is often possible. Examples can remove psychological barriers to success. If others can do this, that means it can be done. As a result, more people try, and more people achieve.

Examples move us toward excellence in at least three ways. First, they inspire us not to settle for mediocrity. Witnessing the extraordinary achievements of others stimulates our aspirations and makes higher goals seem possible. Second, positive examples of men and women accomplishing especially difficult or dangerous tasks can call up our sense of honor and give us the courage to plunge into good causes or risk dangers even when the outcome is uncertain. Third, bad examples can warn us away from certain paths we may be tempted to follow. No one likes to witness or experience failure, but failure happens. When it does, it can be used as a valuable lesson in what to avoid. Let us delve a bit deeper into these three kinds of examples and see what we can learn from them.

Examples Can Inspire Us

All around us, we witness good examples of ordinary people who overcame great challenges and achieved great things. The power of these positive examples is twofold: First, they can make us want to achieve great things, and second, they show us that such excellence is achievable.

Candy Lightner is such an example. She experienced the worst tragedy any parent can endure—the loss of a child. Her beloved thirteen-year-old daughter was killed by a drunk driver. The driver was a repeat offender who had been previously arrested multiple times for DWI. On investigation, Candy learned that, in her state, there were little to no legal consequences for driving while intoxicated. As a result, repeat offenders continued to kill children with drunk driving. Rather than let her grief sink her into depression, Candy Lightner decided to take steps to prevent this tragedy from happening to other families. In her home in 1980, she established an organization she called "Mothers Against Drunk Driving (MADD). Her organization caught on, and her example inspired chapters of MADD to spring up across the country to fight for stricter laws and stiffer penalties to curb the scourge of death by drunk drivers.[17]

Another example is that of J. P. and Paul Norden. These two brothers from Stoneham, Massachusetts traveled to Boston in 2013 to watch the Boston Marathon. They secured prime spots near the finish line when their lives were changed forever. A massive explosion of two bombs set by domestic terrorists killed three people instantly and sent hundreds to the hospital. J. P. and Paul each lost a leg in the blast.

As the Norden brothers recovered in the hospital, they watched others who had lost limbs emerge from the pain and loss only to face a long process of adjustment and heavy expense. Rather than allow their loss to ruin their lives, J. P. and Paul decided to do something

17 Caitlin O'Connell, "15 Ordinary People Who Changed History," Reader's Digest, rd.com, January 30, 2023, https://www.rd.com/list/inspiring-stories-9-ordinary-people-who-changed-history/Accessed April 17, 2023.

positive. After receiving and adjusting to their prosthetic legs, they set up a foundation called A Leg Forever. So far, the foundation has helped more than sixty amputees pay for prosthetics, wheelchairs, and bedside care.[18]

Candy Lightner and the Norden brothers were ordinary people who were inspired by loss and tragedy to do extraordinary things. Few of us face circumstances that call for these kinds of extraordinary and far-reaching results. But we often encounter examples in the course of our daily lives that can inspire us to make a difference in the lives of just one or two people. Just because the example does not lead us to create organizations or foundations doesn't mean it cannot inspire us to do a smaller but significant good. The following two examples demonstrate what I mean.

It was the Christmas season when Tracy Warshal was standing in the payout line at the local supermarket. The man ahead of her told the cashier that he had forgotten his wallet and didn't have enough money to pay for the few items she had rung up. So, without giving it a second thought, Tracy stepped up and paid for the man's items. After the transaction, he asked for her name and left the store. Tracy then paid for her own items and thought no more about the incident.

A month later, Tracy was at her job in the Piedmont Cancer Institute of Georgia when she was called into the company office. The director informed her that an anonymous man, inspired by a kind act she did for him at a supermarket, had just donated $10,000 in her name to the Piedmont Cancer Foundation. Although she had

---

18 Jeff Saperstone, "He and His Brother Lost Their Legs in the Bombing. 'Now, We Get to Help a Lot of People'" nbcboston.com, https://www.nbcboston.com/news/local/norden-brothers-leg-forever/3019280/?utm_source=ActiveCampaign&utm_medium=email&utm_content=%22It+changed+me+for+the+better%22&utm_campaign=04-18-23+Boston+Marathon+bombing+victim%3A+%22It+changed+me+for+the+better%22, April 11, 2023.

given the man only her first name, he had noted that she wore a shirt displaying the name of her employer. So he tracked her down, learned her full name, and made a generous donation in gratitude for her act of kindness. This is truly a story of how a positive example generated exponential results.[19]

Firefighters Tim Young and Paul Hullings had just suffered through a long, grueling night with their team putting out a large warehouse fire in New Jersey. Exhausted, char-smudged, and smelling of smoke, they dragged into a small diner and ordered a hearty breakfast. Waitress Liz Woodward was on duty that morning, and she had heard the sirens and seen news of the nearby fire that the two men had just conquered. After they finished their breakfast, she brought them their check. On it, she had written this:

> Your breakfast is on me today. Thank you for all that you do; for serving others and for running into the places everyone else runs away from. No matter your role, you are courageous, brave, and bold every day! Fueled by fire and driven by courage, what an example you are. Get some rest. –Liz.

Tim and Paul were so touched by Liz Woodward's kind gesture that they wanted to do something for her. They inquired of her coworkers and found that she was struggling to raise money to buy her father a wheelchair-accessible van. The two firefighters quietly went to work. Pooling their own resources to seed the pot, they started a campaign that raised $67,000 for Liz's father—about three times the needed amount. On receiving the gift, the tearful woman said, "This is just one example of how so many people in this world

---

19 Adapted from "The man who thanked a woman for paying for his groceries by donating $10,000 to cancer treatment in her name," bestlifeonline.com, https://bestlifeonline.com/pay-it-forward-stories/, Accessed April 18, 2023.

have incredible hearts, and they pay it forward so the circle keeps on moving."[20] Again and again we see the power of a good example inspiring others to emulate in ways that excel exponentially.

Examples Can Convict Us

Examples of ordinary people who took on large and difficult tasks can ratchet up our courage to do the same. Examples of others making personal sacrifices of their time and careers can inspire us to respond in extraordinary ways to deep needs when we encounter them.

Nicholas Winton inspires us with this kind of example. Winton was born in England in 1909 to Jewish parents who converted to Christianity. In the early days of WWII, he had become a successful stockbroker when he was invited to visit friends in Prague, Czechoslovakia. When he arrived, Nazi Germany was in the process of occupying that nation. When Winton saw the Nazis breaking up Jewish families and sending them off in boxcars, he was drawn to assist in helping smuggle Jewish children out of the country to escape Nazi capture. He returned to England to work with the government on processes to receive refugee children and orchestrate getting them placed in British homes. He overcame formidable obstacles such as finding a solution to the refusal of the Netherlands to allow refugees to cross their borders. When the flow of children increased beyond Britain's capacity to absorb them, he found other countries to accept the overflow. Winton became known as the "British Schindler." He saved the lives of 669 Jewish children, many of whom grew up to be prominent in fields such as medicine, statesmanship, academics, literature, filmmaking, religion, and architecture. His heroic work

---

20 Adapted from "The firefighters who pay their free meal forward," bestlifeonline. com, https://bestlifeonline.com/pay-it-forward-stories/, Accessed April 18, 2023.

went unnoticed for fifty years, but finally, he was widely recognized and honored for his achievements. Among the honors was knighthood bestowed by Elizabeth II.[21]

Examples set by people like Sir Nicholas Winton convict me. They make me want to be on the front lines, to dare the difficult, to plunge into worthy causes and make personal sacrifices of time and effort to help the unfortunate, the destitute, or the hurting. If I encounter an arduous task, Winton's example makes me think twice before I say, "This is too much for me. I'm sure someone else can do it better." The person who can do it best is the person who dares to plunge into it. That could be you. Though you may not want to take on the challenge, you know it needs to be done, and you seem to be in a position to do it. So you grit your teeth and plunge.

Bad Examples Can Warn Us

Just as good examples are loaded with constructive power, bad examples are powder kegs of destructive power. But even bad examples can be useful. They enable us to see what to avoid. The following story is a prime illustration of what a bad example can do. (It was told as a true story about a real person, but because I could not find the original source, I have changed the names.)

Little Kevin's favorite baseball player was Jim Wilson. He wore a Jim Wilson jersey, collected Jim Wilson cards, and memorized Jim Wilson's stats. One day, his mother took Kevin to a fast-food restaurant near the ballpark, and to Kevin's delight, Jim Wilson happened to be sitting in a corner booth eating a burger.

Beside himself with excitement, Kevin got a pen and paper from his mother and walked toward Wilson. Just before he arrived, an

---

21 Nicholas Winton, en.wikipedia.org, https://en.wikipedia.org/wiki/Nicholas_ Winton

older gentleman approached the star to request an autograph. "Are you so blind that you can't see that I'm eating?" growled Wilson. Kevin stopped in his tracks, stunned at what he had heard. As he stood, crestfallen and staring, Wilson glared at him and barked, "Get out of here, kid. How can I eat with you staring at me like that?"

Kevin traded away all his Jim Wilson baseball cards and never wore his Wilson jersey again. When he told the other boys on his Little League team, they also dumped their Wilson paraphernalia. Soon the incident spread on social media to the point that sales of Wilson's cards and jerseys dropped, and sponsors declined to renew their contracts with him.

Your Example is Critical to Your Success

As Jim Wilson's story demonstrates, you are being watched. If you are a leader either at your job, in your church, in an organization, or in your home, the example of what you do always has much more impact than what you say. As Mahatma Gandhi put it, "An ounce of practice is worth more than tons of preaching." Everyone under your leadership is watching you. Each of them knows what your example says, so it is critical that you know as well. That is why you must be intentional in everything you do. Your actions will be the evidence by which they judge you. Those actions must be plumb-line, true and consistent if you expect people to follow you.

The way you treat people reveals your true character. By that I mean the way you treat everybody—not just those above you or those who can do you good or those you want to impress. How do you treat the man who mows your lawn? Your restaurant waitress? The checker at the supermarket? The pesky sales caller on your phone? (Yes, even him!) Your consistency in treating everyone as an equal deserving respect and courtesy is one of the key revealers of your true character. I do not mean you cannot disagree with these people (or even request to be removed from the call list). But it is good to realize, as C. S. Lewis pointed out in *The Weight of Glory*, that the most ordinary human beings we meet are eternal creatures capable of such future glory that if we could see that glory now, we would be tempted to fall down and worship them.

The same principle holds true when you deal with temptations and pressures that test your resolve or your patience. Do you react one way when you think people are looking and another way when you think they are not? You have no basis for expecting others to follow you if your integrity is merely a façade that shows one face in public and another in private. Without consistent character, you forfeit your right to lead and influence others with your example.

A story is told of a woman who brought her young son to the doctor. When he asked what the problem was, she said, "Donnie won't stop eating sweets. I don't give him candy or cookies, but he gets all kinds of sweets at school. I've told him over and over that sugar will ruin his teeth. He won't listen to me, but he will believe you. So just explain to him why he should stop eating sweets."

The doctor sat quietly for a moment, pondering. Then he said to the woman, "Bring Donnie back to me in two weeks."

Two weeks later, the woman had her son in the doctor's office as instructed. After taking Donnie's blood pressure and examining him thoroughly, the doctor sat him down and said, "Donnie, I know you hate to hear it, but you must stop eating sugar. It's bad not only for your teeth, but it could ruin your health in other ways. You won't want to spend your life as a diabetic. If you don't believe me, then I must draw some blood and have it analyzed to show you what I mean." At the sight of the needle, Donnie promised to cease eating sugar.

As Donnie went back to the waiting room, his mother lingered another moment. "Thank you, doctor," she said, "but I can't figure out why you had to wait two weeks to tell my son what you told him today."

The doctor grinned sheepishly and replied, "Well, two weeks ago when you asked me to admonish Donnie, I realized I had been eating way too many sweets. So, that day, I stopped eating sugar and resolved to eat it no more. You see, I realized I wouldn't be a doctor of integrity—or even a man of integrity—if I didn't follow my own advice."[22]

This doctor exemplified the advice of author John C. Maxwell, who said, "If you want to build the kind of credibility that connects with people, then deliver results before you deliver a message. Get out and do what you advise others to do."

The Benefits of Leading by Example

Here I pass along to you five strong benefits that result from leading by example that I adapted from a fine blog by internet writer Iryna Viter.

1. *Positive examples build trust and respect.* Your example tells those who follow you that you are not merely telling them what to do; you are doing it yourself. Your active example builds trust in those around you, which motivates them to become more engaged and leads to more positive results.

2. *Positive examples set the bar of expectation.* What others see you do sets the standard for your expectations. They are more like-

---

22 Adapted from Dr. Alan Zimmerman, "How to Set an Inspiring Example Others Will Follow," drzimmerman.com, https://www.drzimmerman.com/tuesdaytip/how-to-set-an-inspiring-example-others-will-follow, Accessed April 19, 2023.

ly to work hard to be productive when they see you working hard and being productive. When you demonstrate consistent ethics and honesty, you are more likely to see ethics and honesty reflected in those you lead. Modeling the behavior you want to see in others motivates them to follow your example.

3. *Positive examples inspire others.* When those you lead see you pushing yourself to do better, to be more innovative, to seek solutions to problems, and to take on new challenges with relish, they are more likely to imitate your example and accomplish your desires.

4. *Positive examples create a positive environment.* When you consistently treat others with respect, courtesy, and kindness, that treatment will be contagious among your followers. A positive attitude coupled with your willingness to listen, appreciate, praise, and help others achieve their goals contributes to loyalty and cooperative teamwork. When your example creates this kind of environment, people tend to enjoy their work. This leads to greater job satisfaction and employee retention.

5. *Positive examples encourage accountability.* When those around you see you taking ownership of your actions and holding yourself accountable, even to the point of admitting your mistakes and learning from them, your example will greatly increase their respect for you. It will inspire them to do the same, realizing that you understand honest mistakes and will not judge harshly or with recrimination when mistakes are made. You realize that the only people who don't make mistakes are those who don't try to do anything extraordinary.[23]

23 Adapted from Iryna Viter, "How to Lead by Example: The Ripple Effect of Your Actions," runn.io website, February 22, 2023, https://www.runn.io/blog/how-to-lead-by-example.

Setting Examples Can Bring Us Joy

A few years ago, my wife, Lanelle, had to fly to Oklahoma to take care of some matters at our business there. She was disappointed that the trip meant she wouldn't be home on her birthday. On her flight, she began to think about what she could do to make her birthday a positive experience. She came up with the idea of giving each employee $100 with the stipulation that he or she would give the money away to a person who really needed it. The recipient could not be a family member or a friend. It had to be someone they didn't know but was in an unfortunate situation that required money they didn't have. The employees were required to keep a record of the transaction, and later in the week they would be called together to report on their experiences.

On that trip, Lanelle initiated her plan. She gave each employee $100 along with her instructions on how to use it. Later that week, she gathered the employees in a team meeting and had them tell their stories. The stories brought such joy and had such a positive impact on the emotions of the givers that Lanelle decided to make the giveaway a regular event. So, now each time Lanelle and I travel to our Oklahoma business around her birthday, we listen to the heartwarming stories of how they used the money and how it has blessed their personal lives. Most of all, we are blessed by the joy we see in our employees—the kind of joy that always flows from helping others.

I chose to end this chapter with this personal story because it illustrates one benefit of setting a good example that has not yet been emphasized. All the previous example stories point out the advantages we gain in following good examples or the benefits that come to us in our businesses and relationships from setting good examples. But this story demonstrates a truth every bit as deep as the others.

Setting a good example simply demonstrates that we are living our own life by the solid, eternal principles of truth that always bring us real and lasting joy, peace, happiness, freedom, and contentment.

As the stories in this chapter demonstrate, setting good examples almost always results in the multiplication of the good generated by the example. Good examples inspire. They stir our best impulses to emulate the good we see performed in others. This explains why a good example, perhaps better than any other human activity, tends to create a ripple effect that expands outward as people pay the example forward. In other words, setting good examples is among the most productive ways to excel exponentially.

Enhance Your Environment

"You become what you surround yourself with. Energies are contagious. Choose carefully. Your environment will become you."

—Author unknown

In this chapter, I want you to think small. When I use the word "environment," do not think of Planet Earth, but think instead of environments that are much more personal and intimate that affect the way you function in your everyday life. How do the day-to-day settings, situations, conditions, and people that surround you affect your ability to excel?

Let me give you an example of what I am talking about. My wife, Lanelle, and I have some very good friends with whom we have spent countless hours. We camped, cruised, played, worked, cared-for, laughed, and wept together. Perhaps the keyword that defines our relationship with these friends is "elevate." When we are together, we all try to elevate each other in our thoughts and actions. That means we keep the other's good and well-being uppermost in our relationship. The result of this elevation is that when we are together, we create an environment filled with joy, peace, happiness, contentment, and freedom.

Most of us conduct our daily lives in many environments. But for simplification, in this chapter I have chosen to deal with the three most common and primary: home, work/school, and personal. Let us examine these three primary environments to show how they affect us and what can be done to elevate or enhance them.

Enhancing Your Home Environment

The home environment can be divided into two phases: the home you grew up in and the home you live in now. You had little control over the environment of the home you grew up in. Your parents or other adult caretakers were in control. You did not choose your environment, and you could not leave it. That environment, whether good or bad, is now in the past, and it cannot be changed (despite what time-travel movies tell us). Psychologists recognize that our childhood home environment has a huge influence in shaping us into who we are. While it is true that the past cannot be changed, if that early home environment was toxic, its negative effects on you can be overcome.

Signs of a toxic home environment are verbal or physical abuse, uncontrolled anger, manipulative behavior, non-stop drama, unrealistic expectations, and extreme criticism. The result is often fear, guilt, shame, low self-esteem, and helplessness.

Overcoming a toxic home environment. If you grew up in such an environment, the first step in recovering is to recognize its effects on your life. Awareness of the problem is a prerequisite to dealing with it. If the effects are severe, you may need to seek professional counseling to overcome them.

One of the most common and debilitating effects of growing up in a toxic home environment is a feeling of helplessness. If you were abused, criticized, controlled, and forced to do things against your will by people larger and stronger, you may have given up trying to exercise power over your own life. There may have seemed to be no way out, so you quit trying. This condition is called "learned helplessness." According to an article in *Psychology Today*, "Learned helplessness occurs when an individual continuously faces a negative, uncontrollable situation and stops trying to change their circumstances, even when they have the ability to do so." He comes to believe that "nothing he does will help, and therefore he stops trying altogether."[24]

Learned helplessness often imprints in a toxic home environment and carries over into adulthood. But, continues the article, you can overcome learned helplessness by learning new alternate behaviors. "People can push back against learned helplessness by practicing independence from an early age and by cultivating resilience, self-worth, and self-compassion. Engaging in activities that restore self-control can also be valuable."[25]

Brown University offers the following four steps to help overcome the negative effects of a toxic home:

- Make a list of the things you want to change.

- Write next to each behavior the way you would like to behave or feel instead.

---

24 "Learned Helplessness," Psychology Today website, https://www.psychologytoday.com/us/basics/learned-helplessness, Accessed May 9, 2023.

25 Ibid.

- Prioritize the list if you want, and then choose a behavior to start with.

- Practice your desired behavior in place of the one you want to change.[26]

To this list, I would add one more item that will do much to free one from a toxic home environment: forgiveness. As I noted in Chapter 5, forgiveness is one of the most freeing acts you can perform. It removes the weight of resentment. It opens a path to restore broken relationships. It frees one from the recurring habit of reliving traumas of the past.

Creating a positive home environment. Your present home environment is more malleable. It is likely that you had a hand in creating it and thus retain the capacity to change its negative elements or enhance its better ones. Whether you live alone or have a spouse or family, your present home environment plays a significant part in your well-being.

To enhance your home environment, you must maintain courtesy, respect the others in your household, and share tasks. One of the ways Lanelle and I tried to enhance our home environment was by not calling each other or our children negative names. Family members will inevitably disagree at times, but they should take care to do it with consideration for the other's viewpoint. When arguing, never use the word "never" and always avoid the word "always" (as in "You never do this!" or "You always say that!").

When you feel tired and withdrawn and she wants to chat, act better than you feel and engage in the conversation amicably. It is not hypocrisy to act better than you feel; it's attempting to be the kind

---

26 Quoted from "Dealing with Toxic Parents," dfsconsultingph.com, https://dfsconsultingph.com/dealing-with-toxic-parents-negative-home-environment/ Accessed May 9, 2023.

of person we want to be. Acting better than you feel will eventually make you feel better so that it is no longer an act. It's the "fake it till you make it" principle.

These principles and more are summed up in a proclamation by my church offering nine universal principles as foundations for a stable home environment: "Successful marriages and families are established and maintained on principles of faith, prayer, repentance, forgiveness, respect, love, compassion, work, and wholesome recreational activities."[27]

You can see how a home infused with these principles would be a place of happiness and well-being. The attitudes and atmosphere you create in your home will do much to shape you as well as your family. They will stay with you as you enter other environments. Since the home is the basic unit of society, a stable home generates stable people who create stable workplaces and thus a stable society. As you can see, it is a way of excelling exponentially.

Enhancing Your Work Environment

Whether you work in an office, on a construction crew, in the cab of an eighteen-wheeler, in a creative shop, at a computer in your home office, or at some other task or profession, your work environment is where you spend most of your waking hours. If this environment is toxic, it is imperative that you find a way to change it—or leave it.

You can recognize a work environment as toxic when its culture is overwhelmingly negative. The employees are unsatisfied and disgruntled, and productivity is lagging. This negativity is commonly

27 "The Family: A Proclamation to the World," The First Presidency and Council of the Twelve Apostles of the Church of Christ of Latter-Day Saints (Salt Lake City, UT: Intellectual Reserve, Inc., 1995, 2008).

revealed in activities such as distrust, pessimism, gossip and criticism of colleagues and management, flouting company values, and the formation of cliques or in-groups.

The result of these factors is increased illness and absenteeism, high employee turnover, a poor reputation in the industry, poor production quality, and low productivity.

Sometimes the toxic atmosphere in a workplace can be caused by a small clique of employees or even one employee. The negativity spreads throughout the company just as one bad apple spoils the whole barrel. You can usually spot a toxic employee by these telltale signs: negative attitude; refusal to take responsibility for his actions; incessant complaints about company policy and rules; verbally trashing coworkers and supervisors; failure to apply himself to his work; sharing private company information; and being "two-faced," which means presenting a negative, critical attitude among employees and a cooperative attitude toward management. When an employee or group causes toxicity, the solution is obvious; eliminate the cause by discharging the offenders.

The cause of the toxic environment may sometimes lie much deeper. The problem may be caused by the actions or inattention of management or ownership.

Whatever the cause, a toxic work environment can create the same sense of helplessness as a toxic home environment. An example is my friend Jack (not his real name), who worked in a publishing company. He reported directly to a vice president I will call Fred. Fred never expressed satisfaction with Jack's work and often deflated his best efforts with picky criticisms. As a result, Jack assumed he was not pleasing his boss. He grew increasingly unhappy, and though he loved the kind of work he did, he began to dread coming to the office.

One day after Jack had completed a large, complex, and time-consuming project, Fred looked it over and said he thought it would probably be acceptable. It was all Jack could take. He confronted his boss, asking if he wanted him to resign so he could replace him with someone whose work would please him. Fred was surprised, and said, "If I didn't like your work, I would tell you." When Jack asked why he never expressed praise for his work, Fred explained: "Making employees wonder if they are pleasing me keeps them on their toes. They try harder. If I let them know I am pleased, they would become complacent, and their skills would quit growing."

No doubt gushing effusive compliments for every completed project would not be productive. But everyone needs affirmation, and to be deprived of it results not in motivating the employee to try harder; more likely it plunges him into learned helplessness where he says, "The guy can't be pleased, so why try?"

Back in the "dot-com" startup days, I was hired as the sales representative for the Utah territory of an online job-finding company. My boss pushed me hard, using the promise of future "big bucks" once the company went public as the only motivation. He called and emailed me endlessly, putting me under tremendous pressure to bring in new clients and continually adding work to be done immediately with the threat of firing me if I did not perform. I had almost no downtime and lived in constant fear of another email or phone call demanding another pile of work to be completed by yesterday.

I could not thrive in such a negative environment where I had no time to call my own, nor could I change it. So, after ten months, I quit and made the decision to start my own business. Sometimes the only way to enhance your environment is to leave it and create a better one.

Changing the management style displayed in these two examples would have greatly improved the toxic environment these two managers had created. There are many other principles management can follow to avoid or improve a toxic work environment. I offer the following points, which we had employed in our own property management company and found to work quite well:

1. Run your company by the Golden Rule. It tends to become reciprocal and contagious among employees.

2. Require and model professional language and dress standards. Professionalism in communication and appearance tends to inspire professionalism in performance.

3. Embrace fun and humor in the workplace. A light touch oils relationships and promotes goodwill among employees and management.

4. Provide all employees with detailed job descriptions. Clarity of your expectations gives them a sense of security.

5. Take time to listen to employee concerns—both personal and professional concerns. It shows them that you care.

6. Inform employees of major business decisions if possible. Up-front communication dispels destructive rumors and builds trust.

7. Team building exercises at work and outside of work (such as bowling, swimming, etc.).

8. Express gratitude to your employees for work well done, especially when they exceed expectations or meet difficult deadlines.

9. Stick up for employees when they are in the right. It is a simple matter of honoring truth.

10. Maintain an open-door policy of communication between employees and management. Accessibility to you builds trust.

11. Emphasize honesty and integrity and model these qualities to your employees.

Enhancing Your Personal Environment

This is the environment where you spend most of your personal or private time. It includes your time in a car, bus, or subway as you travel to and from work; your time spent on hobbies, sports, church involvement, civic duties, volunteerism, or entertainment. In short, your personal environment includes any activities, mostly discretionary ones, that you engage in outside of home and work.

How we spend our personal time reveals who we really are. As someone said, "Your true character is revealed by what you do when no one is looking." We may play-act or wear masks to hide the truth about ourselves in the workplace or even in the home. But in our private time when we can do whatever we really want and indulge our true desires, we express the truth about ourselves.

We humans are wired to find joy and happiness only when our private and public behaviors become truly integrated. It is what we call *integrity*. Notice the similarity between the two words, "integrated" and "integrity." The idea is that when all facets of our lives are integrated into a unified whole, then we have achieved integrity. We have become in private what we appear to be in public. With this goal in mind, let us look at two facets of our personal environment and discover ways to enhance them.

Enhancing Your Private Time

To maintain good mental and emotional sharpness, I recommend that you avoid what I call "mind contamination." This means limiting TV-watching and time on social media and electronic devices. Let us address both of these areas.

Limit your TV-watching time. To start with, I recommend avoiding most sitcoms. Many of them go for cheap laughs by majoring in stale one-liners and inane storylines accompanied by laugh tracks needed to tell you when you're supposed to laugh. What is worse, most current sitcoms attempt to normalize sexual immorality. Too many of today's movies and miniseries display overt immorality, especially on premium channels.

It is good to keep abreast of current events, and therefore watching a news program regularly is worthwhile. But with several channels presenting 24/7 news, it is easy to get caught up in repetitive cycles and unverified speculation. If you watch news commentators or opinion shows, avoid immersing yourself in a single viewpoint, whether you consider yourself conservative or progressive. Maintain your core convictions, of course, but open yourself up to understanding opposing viewpoints.

Get control of social media. As I noted in Chapter 5, though smartphones and social media were designed to facilitate communication, they tend to do the opposite. They draw people away from direct contact with each other and into the impersonal sphere of the internet, or replace direct, face-to-face contact with electronic communication.

For example, my friend William tells of a road trip he took with a fine and knowledgeable man he hoped to engage in fruitful conversation. The man kept his smartphone turned on the entire trip, and every time it rang—which was often—he said, "Excuse me, I'd better take this." Sustained conversation with him was impossible.

Here are a few healthy habits for controlling your use of social media adapted from an article by Dr. Sannyu McDonald Harris:

- Severely edit your contacts. You cannot be friends with hundreds of people. Cut the list down to those you genuinely care about. Try to ensure most of your conversations occur in real life and use social media only as a secondary tool.

- Severely limit your time on social media. A study published in the *Journal of Social and Clinical Psychology* shows that people who limit their time on social media to under thirty minutes each day report happier moods and feelings. Using the "do not disturb" function or strictly limiting screen time are effective ways to put this practice in place.

- Follow only people and pages that bring you joy. Unfollow, block, or mute content that bothers you, and instead choose to follow things and people that foster positivity.

- Log off social media and shut down your screens about an hour before bedtime.

- Ignore your smartphone when you are out and about. Your smartphone can keep you from living in the moment and enjoying the real world of sights and sounds and personal interactions. When you are doing something fun, do not feel compelled to stop and snap a selfie. Instead, take full advantage of the moment by putting away your phone and being fully present in the real world. Selfie junkies quickly accumulate multiple hundreds of photos on their smartphones—too many to be memorable or useful.

- Take a break! If using social media is making you feel anxious or depressed, take a break from it for a few days. Unplugging helps you recharge your batteries and refocus on what's most important in your life.[28]

Feed your starving mind. For many today, reading books has become a lost art. It is one we need to recover if we want to create a mental environment that will improve our abilities to cope and function with excellence in our other environments. Here are nine benefits of reading that I have gleaned from various websites:

- Reading exercises the brain. Rather than passively receiving information as we do when we watch TV or movies, reading requires cognitive engagement.

- Reading improves memory, both long-term and short-term. Some studies indicate that active readers are less likely to suffer dementia or memory loss as they age.

- Related to the above point, reading improves concentration and the ability to focus by exercising these mental faculties.

- Reading reduces stress and helps you to relax.

- Related to the previous point, reading improves sleep.

- Reading improves literacy. You learn new words, new concepts, and how to relate and compare ideas to those you uncover in other books and in real life.

- Reading increases general knowledge.

- Reading fiction stimulates the imagination and creates empathy with characters, which improves empathy in real life. Fiction also fosters temporary disengagement from the stress of the real world. Think of it as being like a pit stop for a racecar. You

---

28 Condensed and adapted from Dr. Sannyu McDonald Harris, "7 Habits for Social Media," conehealth.com, August 18, 2022, https://www.conehealth.com/services/behavioral-health/7-healthy-habits-of-social-media/

are off the track for a moment, but it is a necessary pause you must take to keep going.

- Finally, reading is a form of very inexpensive entertainment when you compare the price of a book to the hours spent reading it.

Make time for entertainment and relaxation. My points on reading should not be taken to disparage the value of entertainment and relaxation offered by movies, plays, concerts, or watching sports. We all need a break from the routine to relieve stress and unclench our minds. The key is balance. Regulate the use of your personal time wisely, always with the goal of creating environments that will enable you to excel as a well-rounded and productive member of humanity.

Enhance your travel-time environment. If you ride a bus, metro-rail, or subway to work, stimulate your mind or expand your knowledge. Close your laptop, turn off your smartphone, and plunge into an enjoyable book. If you drive to work, listen to an audiobook. In the evening, as you drive home, opt for something lighter that will help you transition from your work environment to your home environment. Listen to music or catch up on the day's news.

Using Your Environment to Excel Exponentially

You cannot control everything in your environments, but, as I have demonstrated in this chapter, you are not helplessly trapped in them. You have the power to improve unpleasant environments and enhance mediocre or even good ones. The essence of this chapter is that the most key factor in your environment is you.

Now, here is the surprising benefit that comes from this process. When you take steps to enhance any one of the three environments addressed here, you will find that you have also enhanced the other two. Enhancing your personal environment will automatically improve your home environment. Enhancing your home environment will automatically improve your work environment—and vice versa. Here's why: As I said above, the key to improving your environment is to improve yourself. In doing this, in effect, you carry a major part of your environment around with you wherever you go. When you leave one environment and enter another, you create an effect like a ripple on a pond. You excel exponentially.

CHAPTER

Embrace Emotions with Empathy

"Empathy is the most mysterious transaction that the human
soul can have, and it's accessible to all of us, but we have to
give ourselves the opportunity to identify, to plunge ourselves in
a story where we see the world from the bottom up or through
another's eyes or heart."

—Sue Monk Kidd

theistic scientist Richard Dawkins believes humans are nothing more than organic machines. He claims we have no free will. Though we think we make freely chosen decisions, we do not really because all our thoughts and actions are dictated by influences on our physical body. These influences include our environment, upbringing, education, experiences, senses, and external stimuli. You may think you freely chose to buy that burger and fries in defiance of your diet to get rid of your belly fat, but according to Dawkins, you had no real choice. Your growling stomach, the whiff of frying onions, and the delicious memory of your last pre-diet burger months ago combined to override that puny thing you call your will and forced you to order the burger combo instead of the salad.

What messes up Dr. Dawkins' philosophy is our emotions. They undermine the idea that we are merely machines. After eating the burger and fries, you may have felt the emotion of guilt. When the machine you call your next-door neighbor backed his car over your petunia bed, the machine you call yourself may have felt the emotion of anger. Emotions often wreak havoc with the efficiency of the machines that Dawkins thinks we are. They can mess things up.

In a little-known 2022 drama-romance movie titled *Beauty and the Billionaire*, the young billionaire, Justin Ross, a man who probably never read Dawkins, runs his corporate empire by the Dawkins principle, insisting that he and his employees are essentially performance machines. He makes no allowance for emotions. The way he puts it is, "Emotions cloud business judgment." He pays his employees well, and in return, he expects instant obedience to his every whim and command. He ignores the fact that his workers are human beings with hopes, fears, ambitions, and desires for happiness.

As the story progresses, however, Justin encounters a temporary employee—a young woman who is not afraid of him and who demonstrates the serious downside of the billionaire's philosophy and management style. His failure to consider his employees' emotions leads not only to constant tension, fear, resentment, and burnout among his workers, but it also jeopardizes advantageous deals with other businesses.

Yet we must admit that there is some truth in what the billionaire says. Emotions can indeed make any environment messy, whether it is the workplace, the home, or any of the other environments we discussed in our previous environment chapter. We have emotions because we are not machines. We are humans infused with feelings, aspirations, hopes, fears, and desires for love, happiness, fulfillment, and success. These feelings sometimes override our judgment and throw efficiency and cooperation out of balance. Emotions and their effects are a fact of life, and we cannot ignore them. We must find a way to deal with them so that they enhance our environment and performance instead of turning order into chaos.

Universal Emotions and Their Effects

Various psychologists classify emotions in diverse ways. Some say there are ten or more basic emotions, while others boil them down to four elemental ones: happiness, sadness, fear, and anger. Other emotions can be subcategorized under these four basic emotions. For example, surprise, disgust, disappointment, pride, shame, excitement, envy, and embarrassment could be called "sub-emotions" or subcategories of the four basic emotions.

Some schools of psychology classify emotions as positive or negative, based on their usual effect on our mental state. Other psychological theorists find this binary classification unhelpful, asserting that all emotions have their place, and even those generally classified as negative, such as fear, have a self-preservation function that alerts us to danger and activates protective responses such as fight or flight. Yet, while we may be reluctant to classify emotions as positive or negative, we cannot escape the fact that emotions not properly dealt with can impair an environment.

Let us begin by looking briefly at how emotions work. At the outset, we must realize that emotions cannot simply be generated at will. You cannot decide to be happy, sad, or angry in a vacuum. Those emotions arise in response to conditions, or they are triggered by events. You feel happy because you got a raise. You feel sad because you lost a friend. You feel fear because a tornado is coming. You feel angry because your wallet was stolen. You can learn to train those emotions so they will not dominate you and dictate negative actions, as soldiers train themselves to perform courageously despite their fear under gunfire. But the emotion cannot simply be willed out of existence—or, for that matter, into existence, either. Method actors who produce tears for the camera often think of an event in their past that triggered sadness. By bringing that event vividly to life in their imagination, they again feel the emotion it triggered and use it to act out the scene.

In essence, emotions are by-products of actions, events, problems, or conditions—whether initiated by us or imposed on us by nature or others. How we process and handle emotions determines their effect on us. It is possible to reach a state of peace that you retain even while feeling emotions such as sadness, anger, grief, or guilt. This state is usually grounded in one's religious conviction and allows for an emotional equilibrium retention, even in the face of personal crises. A critical point to remember is that our own emotions also affect others in our lives—our families, friends, and coworkers. For that reason, emotions need to be managed to ensure harmony in relationships and success in business.

Dealing with Emotions in the Workplace

I have thought about installing at the entrance of my business a box with a sign over it that reads, "Before entering this door, deposit all emotions here." Then I could run my business like the movie billionaire and ignore the emotional side of my workers. But it would not work. Like it or not, employees are going to bring their emotions from home into the workplace. Marriage and family issues, financial strains, grief over losses, or a doctor's diagnosis can trigger feelings of anger, anxiety, frustration, or depression that stick with an employee even on the job. The presence of these emotions often means reduced focus on work, which affects production and product quality. If the employee is unable to manage these emotions, they can spread like a contagion throughout the workplace.

In addition to the emotions that employees bring to work, relationships and frustrations within the workplace can generate their own emotional reactions. These can range from simple personality conflicts to excessive competitiveness, jealousy, rudeness, envy, or resentment that other workers are not pulling their weight.

Although you want to be sensitive and caring, you have a business to run with quotas and deadlines to meet. Somehow, you have got to manage these emotions in ways both effective and sensitive to your employees and customers. In the old movies, when a person broke down under a crisis and collapsed into a blithering basket case, the masterful hero would jerk him up by the collar, give him a couple of slaps on the cheek, and yell harshly, "Come on, man! Snap out of it!" Then the hysterical man would come to his senses, pull himself together, and say, "Thanks, I needed that."

Well, I wish it were that simple, but dealing with real emotions in real life is a bit more complex and nuanced.

Remember, emotions have purpose, and while we want employees to manage them, we do not want to stifle them. When that happens, I am told, the emotion either continues to boil and expand beneath the surface until the pressure builds to the point of explosion. Or it crouches silently in wait, ready to pounce when triggered again.

It is natural for sadness, anxiety, or grief to linger to be carried from home into the workplace. Since we are not machines, we do not have an "off" button that sends the emotion back to the file folder. If you have an employee who is obviously not himself—maybe he is unresponsive to communication or easily irritated—let him know you have noticed and ask if anything is wrong. You need not probe for a detailed response, but simply knowing he is dealing with a problem should be enough to enable coworkers to cut him some slack. And it will help him to know that he is being understood.

Some disruptive displays of emotion will inevitably occur even in the best of environments, and we need not try to manage minor incidents of common irritation or disagreement. The problem comes when these emotions continue, expand, or get out of hand. Remember, as much as you may wish you could staff your workplace solely with robots, you are stuck with humans (for now), and humans are going to emit emotions just as machines emit noise. So let us look at a few steps you can take to manage the disruptive effects of emotions that occur in your environment.

1. *Establish firm conduct rules.* These rules include prohibitions against shouting, screaming, the use of bad language, and gossip that casts a negative light on other employees or management. Do not allow employees to argue loudly or extensively, causing disruption and distraction among other workers.

2. *Stay alert to intercept undermining or disruptive rumors.* They will spread in almost every company. "Bob heard there are going to be layoffs." "Mary said budget cuts are coming." "I heard that John, who's doing the same job we're doing, is making 20 percent more than we are." Have private meetings with

employees who spread these rumors and warn them against continuing.

3. *Be what you expect your employees to be.* Keep your emotions under control. Reflect positivity. Set an example of diligence, focus, and good will. Express appreciation for employee diligence, dedication, and positivity.

4. *Be understanding.* Show empathy (as we will discuss in greater depth below), particularly for employees dealing with serious problems, griefs, or losses in their homes or personal lives. Encourage them to express their needs, give them reasonable time off, and call them at home to check on their well-being.[29]

5. *Provide emotional ventilation.* All sorts of things in a work environment can cause emotions to fester. A problem client, technical snags, deadline pressures, or misunderstood company directives. Set up regular group meetings with your employees to give them a forum where they can vent freely and voice their feelings. In turn, you can address reasonable concerns, and you may even learn things that lead you to make changes in policy.

The Goal: Generating a Positive Work Environment

We have emotions put down or relegated to the margins so often that we tend to forget they must have a high value, or we would not have them. So just what is the value of emotions?

---

29 It is beyond the scope of this chapter to give detailed information about dealing with any of the problems mentioned in point 4. But dealing with grief is such a sensitive and difficult issue that I want to pass on to you a good resource that offers helpful information. It is titled "Bereavement in the Workplace" and provides a set of excellent guiding principles and steps for dealing with a bereaved employee in the workplace. It is offered by The Greater Metropolitan Cemeteries Trust and can be accessed here: https://www.gmct.com.au/resources/bereavement-in-the-workplace

Throughout this book, I have pointed out that true excellence is achieved by pursuing goals that bring joy, peace, happiness, freedom, and contentment. A billion-dollar bottom line is meaningless if you have no joy. The pride of running a Fortune 500 company is meaningless if you have no peace. Widespread fame is meaningless if you have no contentment. It is through the emotions that we experience a life worth living. What would life be like without the emotion of joy? While we know that love should be grounded in commitment, the emotions we feel because of love are among the most wonderful things a human can experience. As French philosopher Blaise Pascal said, "The heart has its reasons which reason knows nothing of... It is the heart which perceives God and not the reason." Pascal was telling us that the heart—poetically regarded as the seat of human emotions—is the home of happiness, faith, joy, and love. Perhaps we could put it this way: Reason guides us to the real and the true, but then it turns the wheel over to the emotions to experience the joy of what reason has discovered.

The one universally desired emotion is happiness. So, our task for ourselves and for those in our environment is to create conditions that foster happiness. What makes you happy? What makes your employees happy? What makes your family happy? The details will vary with each individual, but the following list identifies the overarching needs that when met provide happiness for almost everyone:

- A sense of belonging, of being part of something significant.

- A sense of purpose—making a positive contribution to the whole.

- The opportunity to exercise one's skills and talents.

- The recognition or reward for performance.

- Positive personal relationships—friendship, love.

- A balance of amusement, recreation, and entertainment.

- A sense of security.

- Physical and mental health and well-being.

- Giving to others or helping others in need.

So, to excel exponentially, we must not follow the advice of the movie billionaire and exclude emotions to prevent their potentially negative effects. Emotions will happen, excluded or not. Rather than try to ban or suppress them, we must foster an environment where emotions can flourish positively and not cloud judgment or disrupt the work environment. We must encourage a sense of positivity that inspires workers to rise above the effect of emotions that may momentarily beset them, opening a path for them to enjoy the life of excellence we try to create for ourselves and those we are charged to serve.

The Solution: Empathy

It may surprise you that I am proposing empathy as the solution to understanding and managing emotions arising in any environment. You may think I am urging you to use an emotion to manage emotions. But think of empathy not as an emotion but as an act of will that generates insight into emotions. Empathy recognizes and takes into account human emotional needs. When we exercise empathy, we try to think of ourselves as experiencing the situation that's troubling the other person. It means seeing her difficulties from the inside, imagining her pains, and feeling her emotions.

Empathy is beautifully illustrated in this story Stephen Covey tells about riding in a quiet, peaceful subway on a Sunday when suddenly...

... a man and his children entered the subway car. The children were so loud and rambunctious that instantly the whole climate changed.

The man sat down next to me and closed his eyes, apparently oblivious to the situation. The children were yelling back and forth, throwing things, even grabbing people's papers. It was very disturbing. And yet, the man sitting next to me did nothing.

It was difficult not to feel irritated. I could not believe that he could be so insensitive as to let his children run wild like that and do nothing about it, taking no responsibility at all. It was easy to see that everyone else on the subway felt irritated, too. So finally, with what I felt was unusual patience and restraint, I turned to him and said, "Sir, your children are really disturbing a lot of people. I wonder if you couldn't control them a little more?"

The man lifted his gaze as if to come to a consciousness of the situation for the first time and said softly, "Oh, you're right. I guess I should do something about it. We just came from the hospital where their mother died about an hour ago. I don't know what to think, and I guess they don't know how to handle it either."

Can you imagine what I felt at that moment? My paradigm shifted. Suddenly I *saw* things differently, and because I *saw* differently, I *thought* differently, I *felt* differently, I *behaved* differently. My irritation vanished. I didn't have to worry about controlling my attitude or my behavior; my heart was filled with the man's pain. Feelings of sympathy and compassion flowed freely. "Your wife just died? Oh, I'm so sorry! Can you tell me about it? What can I do to help?" Everything changed in an instant.[30]

The moment Stephen Covey understood the man's situation, he employed empathy. His sympathy and compassion placed him vicariously in the other man's position. He felt the man's grief, which enabled him to understand why the poor fellow was not functioning well at the moment as a father. Empathy led Mr. Covey to do more than just feel. He reached out and offered help. That is what authentic empathy does.

How important is empathy? A recent Forbes study says it is the most important of all leadership skills. Empathy is the ability to understand another person by imagining his problem as your own and thinking how you would feel or act in a similar situation. Empathy means being approachable and human. You don't hole up in your office with the door closed. You mingle. You get to know your people so you can understand their thinking and their problems.

Empathy differs from pity and sympathy. Pity feels sorry for the person suffering, but it does not get personally involved in it. Sympathy goes one step further and involves feeling: "I feel your pain, and I'm sorry you are experiencing it." Empathy takes the next step forward. It not only feels the pain of the other person, but it also takes steps to identify with the sufferer enough to step up and see what can be done to help him.

Becoming an Empathetic Leader

So what makes an empathetic leader? The bottom line is that he's a person who cares as much about his people as he does about

---

30 Stephen R. Covey, *The 7 Habits of Highly Effective People* (New York: Simon & Schuster, 1989, 2004), 38–39.

their output. He's good not only at getting the work done efficiently, he's also a good people person. In fact, he gets the work done
efficiently at least partly because he is a people person.

If you are not already an empathetic leader, I cannot offer a
magic potion for you to drink that will transform you overnight.
Any change in habits or character takes intentionality and time. You
have first got to want it, and then you've got to put forth the effort
to get it. Here I offer four significant action steps you can follow to
help you become a more empathetic leader in your business, your
home, your church, or any environment where you have leadership
responsibility.

1. *Listen first; speak second.* The empathetic leader projects an attitude that says, "This conversation is not about me; it's about
   you. I want to hear what you think, how you feel." Then after
   you have listened and expressed appropriate responses to what
   you've heard, you can express your own perspective. This approach lets the other person feel that you really care about her,
   her viewpoint, and her feelings.

2. *Show your own vulnerability.* Share a story about yourself in
   an analogous situation. Relating a mutual experience promotes the idea that you really do understand what he's going
   through, which allows him to relate to you better. You've been
   there, done that.

3. *When necessary, use your imagination to replace experience.* You
   cannot, of course, experience every possible situation your employees may find themselves in. If what they relate to you is
   something you have not experienced, then call up your imagination and try to put yourself in a similar situation so you
   can feel something like what they are feeling. Remembering a

scene from a movie might be helpful, or something you read in fiction or a biography.

4. *Avoid making assumptions or rushing to judgment.* Most of us typically approach any problematic situation with some preconceived idea of what likely happened and why. The empathetic leader must overcome that tendency and adopt the legal presumption that everyone is innocent until proven guilty. Approach the situation with an open mind. Don't make a judgement until you've thoroughly heard and grasped all the facts.[31]

The central idea behind all these insights and suggestions is that, whatever business you are in—or for that matter, whatever environment you are in, whether it's the workplace, home, with friends, or at church—you must deal with people. I know we keep hearing that robots and AI will soon make humans obsolete, but until that day comes (and do not hold your breath waiting for it), you are stuck with people and their emotions. Real people are not the automatons that Dawkins thinks we are or the emotionless bootlickers the movie billionaire wanted his minions to be. We are dealing with real people with real hopes, ambitions, loves, joys, and troubles—people who churn out real emotions that must be taken into account.

I think the bottom-line meaning that underlies all this is superbly expressed in Charles Dickens' beloved book, *A Christmas Carol.* The story opens with old Ebenezer Scrooge, who disdains emotions, hates people, runs his business by the principle that profit excludes all other considerations, treats his one, overworked employee like a slave, pays him starvation wages, and threatens dismissal for any infraction of his miserly rules.

---

31 https://www.shrm.org/resourcesandtools/hr-topics/employee-relations/pages/why-empathetic-hr-leaders-are-more-effective.aspx

On Christmas Eve, Scrooge is visited by the ghost of his former partner, Jacob Marley, who has been dead for seven years. Marley is condemned to wander and mourn his wretched life throughout eternity. He has come to warn Scrooge that unless he changes his ways, he will suffer the same fate.

"But you were always a good man of business, Jacob," says Scrooge, meaning he and Marley had shared the same business philosophy—stash away all the cash you can.

"Business!" cried the Ghost, wringing its hands again. "Mankind was my business. The common welfare was my business; charity, mercy, forbearance, benevolence, were all my business!"

Marley's point is that business is not really our business; "Mankind is our business." Yes, we must operate our companies in a way that makes a living for us and our employees. And that is the point: we work to make *a living*, not to make more money. We work to achieve our hopes, to meet our needs, and to create a life of happiness—not to accumulate more stuff, beat the competition, or win admiration for our success. As Marley reminds us, it is all about people, and that means dealing with real live beings with real talents, real flaws, and real emotions.

The movie billionaire, Jacob Marley, and Ebenezer Scrooge all succeeded in business. But it was a one-dimensional success. It was all about accumulation to benefit the self, piling up cash, engorging bank accounts, and swallowing up companies simply to satisfy one's insatiable ego or power lust.

In the earlier part of the twentieth century, John D. Rockefeller was possibly the richest man in America. At the height of his success, a reporter who wondered why he kept pushing so hard to expand his conglomerate empire asked him, "What will it take for you to be satisfied?" Rockefeller replied, "Just a little bit more."

If the unending quest for just a little bit more is the measure of your success, it is a very one-dimensional success. It is centered on you, your personal wants, your material accumulation, your security, your ego. You may be succeeding financially, but you are not excelling or succeeding exponentially. Your success is wrapped up in a tight package that includes little other than self.

To excel exponentially, your success must break out of the bank vault and rise above the bottom line. The effects of your efforts must be planted in your own life and in the lives of others in ways that promote not simply financial success, but success in living a life of joy, peace, happiness, freedom, and contentment. That is the only way to break success out of its one-dimensional focus on financial accumulation. That breaking out leads not merely to success, but to exponential excellence, because it flows outward into every area of life. It is excellence that does not merely accumulate; it radiates. It sows seeds not only in your own life, but also in the lives of those in your environment. Those seeds also sprout into other environments and extend into other lives, on and on *ad infinitum*. That is what it means to excel exponentially.

Employ Essential Ethics

"Ethics is knowing the difference between what you have a right to do and what is right to do."

—U.S. Supreme Court Justice Potter Stewart

Bobby came home from school quite confused. "Dad," he said. "Today the teacher taught us about morals and ethics, but I still can't figure out the difference. Can you explain it to me?"

"Certainly, son," replied the father. "You know I'm a lawyer, so let's say an elderly lady hires me to write her will. It's a simple will, so I gave her an invoice for only $100. But being no longer mentally sharp, she writes the check for $1,000. The moral question is, do I tell the lady about her mistake? The ethical question is, do I tell my partner?"

Before we get into this chapter, I need to give you a better explanation of morality and ethics than this father gave to his son. Morality is a code of behavior based on the absolute principles of right and wrong. Ethics, on the other hand, focuses on the decision-making process for determining how to align one's actions to the moral absolutes of right and wrong. This sometimes involves weighing the pros and cons of competing interests. To sum it up, morality is the standard by which we make our ethical decisions, and ethics is the process of applying morality consistently in specific situations.

Here is a real-life example. You would expect a highly successful retail chain like the CVS Health Corporation to be scrupulously determined not to sell products that would damage their customers' health. But for the first forty-seven years of CVS's existence, all their stores sold a full range of tobacco products. In 2014, however, CVS management apparently experienced an ethical epiphany. They removed all tobacco products from their stores across the nation and have not sold them since. This is an example of an ethical decision because CVS chose to do what was right and consistent with its moral commitment to health despite the resulting loss of revenue. As it turned out, the company's risk paid off. CVS' overall profitability increased, even without tobacco revenues.

A positive outcome, however, is not always the inevitable result of ethical decisions. There is sometimes a cost. In this chapter, I want to show that while practicing ethics can sometimes be costly, it is always worthwhile in the long run. I am convinced that one will never achieve true excellence without being scrupulously ethical.

The Six Essential Ethical Characteristics

I have identified six essential elements that one can employ to become scrupulously ethical in the workplace. They are integrity, honesty, confidentiality, loyalty, reliability, and etiquette. Let us explore these values one by one.

Integrity

As I explained in Chapter 7, when the ethics you display reflect the deep truth about what you are at heart, we call it integrity. This means you hold to a high standard of morality, and your actions are consistent with that standard. Who you are and what you do are fully *integrated*, which means, as is evident in the similarity of the two words, you reflect *integrity*. You act the same in the dark as in the light, in private as in public, at home as at work, with golfing buddies as at church, whether anyone is looking or not. You are the same person acting by the same set of moral values, whatever situation or environment you are in.

I have a friend who prefers to pay with cash rather than using a card. He once received twenty dollars too much in change after paying at a restaurant. While leaving, he checked his change and discovered the error. He turned around and returned the twenty, saying, "It seems you gave me too much in change." The cashier was grateful but shocked. "Why didn't you just keep it?" he asked. My friend responded, "I don't want to have to live with a thief."

Of course, the thief my friend would have had to live with was himself. But because his morality and his actions were integrated, he exercised integrity.

Several years ago, Lanelle and I hired two experienced people to manage an apartment complex handled by our property management franchise in Oklahoma City. These individuals reported a high vacancy rate in these apartments, blaming it on the high crime and drug use in the area. After a while, we began to suspect that something was not quite right in their reports, so we made a trip to Oklahoma to investigate.

We found that the apartments had actually been filled with tenants. Our managers were collecting the rents in cash (against company policy), pocketing most of the money, and sending Lanelle false reports. Lanelle uncovered additional evidence of fraud and embezzlement totaling several thousand dollars, which we presented to the police. They arrested these two, but that did not solve the problem we faced. Integrity demanded that we pay back the apartment complex owners who had lost revenues under our franchise's management of their property. This incident occurred early in our business when we had very little liquidity. We had to cash out our retirement fund and savings, but we paid back every penny due to our clients.

We never told the property owners that we had been defrauded and had to make up their losses out of our own funds. Over time, our franchise was honored as one of the top ten in the nation. We paid a severe cost to maintain integrity, but it paid off in the long run. This experience demonstrated that being ethical in business will go a long way toward helping one to excel exponentially.

Honesty

If you love football as much as I do, you know that when a receiver stretches out to catch a pass, brings it into his body, and falls to the turf, it's often hard to tell whether he maintained control of the ball. If not, he typically will quickly cup his hands under the ball to hide the fact that it actually touched the ground, invalidating the reception. Most fans do not even give this deception a second thought. We take it for granted that this is what players will do. But in a world where ethical behavior was the norm, no receiver would ever attempt such deception, and we would be appalled that anyone would even try it.

American golfer Bobby Jones gave us an example of how this ethical norm should look. Jones was highly popular about a century ago when he won many national and international golf matches. While playing the eleventh hole in the 1925 U.S. Open in Boston, his club accidentally brushed the grass, causing his ball to move slightly. Bobby reported the infraction to the officials, saying he had violated Rule 18. They declined to impose the one-stroke penalty because they did not see the violation. But Bobby insisted until they gave in. Because of the penalty, he tied the game instead of winning by one stroke, forcing a playoff. which he lost. Amazed sportswriters praised him for his honesty, to which he replied, "You might as well praise me for not robbing banks."

Bobby Jones simply told the reporters that honesty should not be exceptional. It should be our default mode in all circumstances. Honesty means being completely truthful, straightforward, and above board in all your dealings with all people— competitors, associates, customers, suppliers, employees, employers, friends, acquaintances, and family. Even when it hurts, as in the case of Bobby Jones.

We all slip and make mistakes, of course, and the common human tendency is to cover them up, as football receivers do, or shift the blame. Ethical behavior, however, demands that we own up honestly to our errors and take full responsibility for them. More often than not, honest admission even of costly mistakes will be forgiven if you have built a prior reputation for being truthful—as the following story demonstrates.

As a teenager, I often went with a couple of friends to a local amusement park to play the Skee-Ball machine. When you accumulated enough points, you won a prize of a fuzzy stuffed animal, which we would give to whatever girls we were pursuing at the time. The more points you earned, the larger the animal you would win.

Criminal geniuses that we were, we learned to manipulate the machine to award us points we did not actually earn so we could win the largest prizes. As if that was not bad enough, we learned to retrieve our quarter before the machine sucked it into its box. So, we fooled the machine and operator into thinking we played two games, and thus we won two stuffed animals for the price of one quarter. (I won't reveal our dastardly secret for fear of tempting you, my dear reader, into a life of crime.)

Well, thirty years later, my conscience finally woke up from its Rip Van Winkle slumber and inflicted severe guilt on me. I called the amusement park (which was still run by the same family), confessed my despicable sin, and said I wanted to repay the money I had cheated them out of. The manager would not hear of it. He forgave me and said what happened thirty years ago was best forgotten. But my guilt lingered, so I devised a solution. I treated my two youngest boys to a day at that amusement park. We played game after game for hours until I was sure that we had paid back many times more than the amount I had swindled as a teenager.

Confidentiality

For most of us, the challenge to the ethical principle of confidentiality usually involves just the simple determination to keep a secret. Here is an example you have probably experienced: Your friend pulls you to the side, looks around, lowers her voice, and says, "What I am about to tell you was told to me in strict confidence, so you must promise that you will not pass it on or reveal it to anyone." Did you listen to the secret, or did you tell your friend that she, herself, was violating the very principle she was demanding that you honor?

Confidentiality is required not just on a personal level, but also in our business dealings—during sensitive contract negotiations, with our employees and employers, with insider knowledge of publicly traded stocks. As part of a company management team, you may have received confidential information about an impending layoff. To reveal this information prematurely would create uncertainty and panic, and likely affect job performance. But these practical considerations are not the real reasons for keeping confidence. The underlying reason is simple integrity. You keep confidence simply because it is the ethical thing to do.

When people share their confidential information with you, they are paying you a great compliment. They are demonstrating their respect for you. They trust you, and they believe you have character and integrity sufficient to warrant their depositing valuable information into your keeping. Their esteem of you is a rich treasure that you should value greatly and protect. When you violate that confidence, the resulting loss of trust and respect is almost impossible to recover. That is why it is so critical to your character to keep to yourself anything that has been told or revealed to you in confidence.

Loyalty

Author and ethicist Eric Felton wrote, "Without loyalty there can be no love. Without loyalty, there can be no family. Without loyalty, there can be no friendship. Without loyalty, there can be no commitment to community or country."[32] Mr. Felton is right; loyalty

---

32 Quoted from Meghan Jones, "Loyalty Quotes That Will Help Build Honesty and Trust," *Reader's Digest* website, May 17, 2023, https://www.rd.com/article/loyalty-quotes/

is the master key to the cohesion and bonding of people, whether it is a love relationship of two, a friendship of a few, a group of several, a community of thousands, or a nation of millions.

One of the best-known examples of loyalty is the development within a platoon of soldiers. Men in battle bond tightly because they know their lives depend on cooperation and care for each other. Loyalty can work the same way to benefit a company. Employees who care about their company and their fellow workers will be more effective, productive, and less inclined to leave. The question for every management team is, "How do I achieve this kind of loyalty?" The answer is found in the simple Golden Rule: Be as loyal to your employees as you want them to be to you.

We can see one of the best examples of this kind of loyalty in the story of Ken Iverson, the CEO of the steel manufacturing company NUCOR in the 1980s and 1990s. NUCOR paid its workers a competitive weekly wage and added a bonus based on annual profits. Often the bonus was more than the workers' annual income. Before the mid-1990s, the average NUCOR worker income was over $50,000, quite high for the time. In addition, the company gave all employees $1,500 annually for each child they had in college.

Iverson ran his multi-billion-dollar corporation on a lean budget with no showy expenses such as corporate jets or elaborate corporate offices. His management staff only consisted of 22. He allowed no executive perks such as reserved parking spaces or special benefits, and he answered his own phone whenever he was in his office. Thus he was able to invest much more into his workforce than most companies.

Because of Iverson's emphasis on employees, NUCOR had a strict no-layoff policy. In the only year when the company's earnings plunged severely, he was forced to make a temporary cut in employee pay. It was an equally applied, across-the-board cut of almost 20 percent. When the necessity of the cut became inevitable, Iverson sent a letter to all employees apologizing for the cut and placing the blame on himself. He explained that he was cutting his own income by 60 percent and promised to restore normal wages as soon as the financial crisis was over. As a result, NUCOR retained almost 100 percent of its workforce and, with loyal employees pulling together, emerged from the crisis quickly. The NUCOR story illustrates how cultivating loyalty in a group creates motivation to achieve the goals of the group.

Before leaving the ethic of loyalty, I must offer one warning. Loyalty, perhaps more than any other ethic, is subject to conflicting feelings. This occurs when loyalty to a person or group overrides commitment to moral truth. Loyalty can lead one to violate principles of ethics or morality.

Reliability

Back when Tom Landry was the coach of the Dallas Cowboys, he once commented on the consistent reliability of his great fullback, Walt Garrison. "When you need four yards, Walt will get you four yards. When you need eight yards, Walt will get you four yards."

According to Sterling W. Sill, "Reliability is a most wonderful virtue. We should cultivate it. We should be consistent about the things we do, so that others will know they can count on us."[33] Reliability is associated with words like trustworthy, dependable, consistent, responsible, and faithful. To be reliable is to do what you say

---

33 Quoted from Meghan Jones, "Loyalty Quotes That Will Help Build Honesty and Trust," *Reader's Digest* website, May 17, 2023, https://www.rd.com/article/loyalty-quotes/

you will do. You show up when needed. You are always on time. You are always prepared, ready, and equipped to do the task at hand.

Of course, interruptions, accidents, and unexpected circumstances can interfere with our best efforts to be reliable. When these things happen, we must do our best to inform those who are depending on us that we will not be able to do our part. Then, after the fact, we must do all we can to correct, repair, or resolve any problem that may have been caused by our failure.

There is a story about a wealthy Englishman who had bought a Rolls Royce automobile and was driving it in rough terrain through the Swiss Alps. After hearing a loud snap, he found that an axle had broken. He hiked to a nearby phone and called the Rolls Royce dealership in England. Within just a few hours, a private plane carrying three mechanics and a new axle arrived at the airport. They met him in a rented car, drove him to the site of the breakdown, and made the repair.

The man returned to England, and, after waiting weeks, he called the Rolls Royce company and asked why they had not sent an invoice. The company replied, "There must be some mistake. Rolls Royce automobiles do not break axles."

Rolls Royce's reputation for reliability was high not only because of their cars' exceptional dependability, but also because they protected that reputation with equally reliable service.

Etiquette

We tend to think about etiquette in terms of mannerly rules such as which fork to use, not to slurp your soup, how to address a queen or president, whether to shake or kiss a woman's hand, avoiding certain words in polite company, saying "pardon me," "I'm sorry," and "thank you," and keeping quiet in a library or theater.

However, Emily Post, the quintessential expert on etiquette, had this to say about what etiquette really means: "Nothing is less important than which fork you use. Etiquette is the science of living. It embraces everything. It is ethics. It is honor."[34]

Emily Post makes a good point. The truth about etiquette lies behind all those mannerly acts. Real etiquette involves attempting at all times to ensure that the people in our presence feel at ease. The rules of etiquette are merely external guidelines for how to accomplish this goal. Etiquette can be characterized as the visual manifestation of the morality and ethics you embody. It is ethical behavior on display, bubbling up to the surface from one's deeper integrity and revealed in the small ways we treat people as well as the large.

It seems that etiquette addresses in a particular way some of the issues I have discussed already in this book. Etiquette involves empathy. It displays concern for the feelings and comfort of others. Etiquette involves emotions. We want to reduce discomfort and un- certainty on the part of others. Etiquette involves the suppression of the ego. We want the other person to feel equal and validated in our presence.

To excel exponentially, etiquette must not be like a suit we wear only when we feel the need to be presentable. It must become ingrained within our psyche, like a habit. It must become part of who we are so the self we present to others is not merely an act we perform in public. Once we establish consistent etiquette in our lives, we are who we are in all environments—at work, at home, at a party, at a dinner, or at play.

---

34 Emily Post, as quoted in Forbes Quotes, forbes.com, https://www.forbes.com/quotes/2646/, accessed June 22, 2013.

There are many rules and ideas about etiquette, but I have compiled a list of seven that seem to further the goals that etiquette is designed to achieve:

- Say "thank you" and "please."

- Give genuine compliments.

- Don't be boastful, arrogant, or loud.

- Listen before speaking.

- Speak with kindness and caution.

- Do not criticize, condemn, or complain.

- Be punctual.

I think the value of these items is self-explanatory, so I will not take the space to elaborate on them. Instead, I want to close this chapter with three applications of etiquette that I think are sorely needed in our particular time and culture.

Etiquette and Personal Integrity

We've all known a colleague who at work is the most calm, mannerly, cooperative, and pleasant person you could imagine. But when he gets home, he sheds the façade of manners and reverts to just "being himself." His reasoning is that home should be a refuge from the demands of business and society—a place where you do not have to wear a mask or pretend to be something other than what you really are. As a result of this self-centered attitude, the family suffers from his rudeness, his dismissal of others, his desire to be left alone, and his demands for peace and quiet. He becomes a tyrant.

To display personal integrity, we must be the same person in all environments, including home, work, church, and anywhere else. We must practice the principles of etiquette in our relationships with those around us until they become second nature. Once this happens—that is, once a person develops the habit of etiquette to the point that it becomes an engrained characteristic—then he can rightly go home and simply "be himself." For then the self he is at work is the same self he is at home. He has an integrated personality. He is the same person wherever he goes, and he never has to put on an act to seem better than he feels—or better than he is.

Etiquette and Social Media

Get on any social media site and you will think America is on the brink of another civil war. What you find is an uncivil war of words raging constantly. Much of social media has become a heated battleground, and the primary weapon is rudeness. It is possible to disagree without being disagreeable. Or at least, it was before social media poisoned the atmosphere that civil debate once thrived in.

None of us as individuals can end the war raging in social media, but we can become non-combatants. We can use civility and normal courtesy in our replies, even (or rather especially) to those who display anger and rudeness toward us. We may not fix the problem, but by refusing to become a part of it, we may influence others out there in cyberspace to be a bit more civil in posting comments.

Etiquette and Everyday Language

Are you as bothered as I am by how crude everyday language has become? Swear words, once forbidden in polite conversation, are now commonly used everywhere. When a friend of my acquaintance was asked why he uses profanity, he replied, "For impact. It strengthens language, adding emphasis to drive home your point."

Not so. The man mistook shock value for strength. Shock value fades quickly. After a few repetitions, profanity no longer shocks;

it merely bores. Swear words become clumsy crutches for speech crippled by lazy vocabularies. The half-dozen common swear words have specific definitions, all associated with judgment, excrement, and crude sexuality. Yet they are thrown indiscriminately into discourse on any subject, displacing helpful descriptive words and robbing conversation of vividness and specificity.[35]

In our businesses, we strongly encourage the use of clean language devoid of swear words. It is simply a matter of considerate etiquette, of respect for others in a mutual environment where a wide variety of sensibilities could easily be offended by crass speech. It is unprofessional and unnecessary. Our speech should consistently reflect our commitment to morality and ethical behavior as prescribed in common etiquette. It is a matter of integrity.

In our home, we established a rule that no swear words would be spoken. One morning in our family scripture study, it was my son Caden's turn to read. His assigned verse was Mormon 2:13, which says, "But behold this my joy was vain, for their sorrowing was not unto repentance, because of the goodness of God; but it was rather the sorrowing of the damned, because the Lord would not always suffer them to take happiness in sin." He paused before reading the word "damned." I asked why he stopped, and he said the next word was a swear word that he was not supposed to say. I told him it was okay to say it when reading it as part of the scriptures. So he started the verse again and read it to completion. Then, to have a little fun with Caden, I got after him for saying a swear word. My attempt at humor went over his head, and he got upset. I had to apologize for my teasing.

---

35 Adapted from Thomas Williams, "The Inanity of Profanity," in the magazine *The Christian Appeal*, March 2023.

To excel in business, family relationships, or any environment where you are in constant contact with people, etiquette is a necessity. People quit jobs because of the rudeness of their employers. Employees are fired because of rudeness. Families become estranged, and often it is not because of any deep or critical issue dividing them; it is simply because people do not realize how critical is the need to treat each other with respect and courtesy. That is, with ordinary etiquette. We are not exempt from using courtesy and etiquette just because we are dealing with people who know us well and thus should overlook our slackness in exercising these critical graces.

Excelling Exponentially with Ethics

In this chapter, have you picked up on the central core of what ethics is about? Essentially, it is about how we treat others. It is summarized in the Golden Rule. We apply these people-principles daily in our ethical decisions and demonstrate them in our etiquette. These principles mean that negotiations should be conducted with the expectation of a win-win outcome rather than attempting to get the best of the other party. Pricing should be fair and honest. Success should be shared, both in terms of acknowledgment of participation and financial reward where appropriate. Dealings with employees should be conducted impartially without favoritism or unfairness.

What is the payoff? You are probably aware of what is called the butterfly effect in chaos theory, which says that the amount of air displaced by the wings of butterflies creates a domino effect that eventually triggers hurricanes. It's actually a metaphor and doesn't mean that literally. Small actions combine and expand to create enormous effects. Seemingly insignificant acts of ethical behavior will expand exponentially throughout your environment and will do much to pave your path to excellence.

10

Earn Economic
Excellence

*"If we command our wealth, we shall be rich and free.
If our wealth commands us, we are poor indeed."*

—Edmund Burke

In the classic movie *Fiddler on the Roof*, a drifting young radical wanders into the poverty-stricken Russian village of Anatevka. There he encounters the main character, Tevye, a poor milkman with five daughters who is struggling against great adversities to make ends meet. The radical notices Tevye's evident craving to be wealthy and warns him that money is a curse. Tevye looks up into the heavens and replies, "May the Lord smite me with it. And may I never recover!"

The Good, the Bad, and the Ugly about Money

The Bible tells us that, "For the love of money is a root of all kinds of evil" (1 Timothy 6:10 NKJV). That passage is often misconstrued to say that *money* is the root of all evil. That is not so. Money is neither good nor evil. It is a morally neutral medium of exchange invented to facilitate trade by replacing the cumbersome practice of barter. Money can be used for good or evil, but when it is used for evil, the evil is not in the money itself but in the aims of the person misusing it. As Ayn Rand said, "Money is only a tool. It will take you wherever you wish, but it will not replace you as the driver."

Money is indeed only a tool, but it is a very useful one. It enables us to live—to buy food, clothing, transportation, and shelter for ourselves and our families. But it is all too easy to let money get out of control and yield to the temptation of wanting more—more things or bigger, better, and showier things. Or more security, more control, more power, or just more for the sake of having more.

We use money to gain the power to do what we want or to gain control over our lives or even over the lives of others. But when we use money for these less-than-noble ends, it often reverses its power and gains control over us. To illustrate how this reversal can happen, I will tell you of a little drama a friend of mine saw played out in nature. He happened to be watching as a mud-dauber wasp landed on the funnel-shaped web of a spider and got caught in it. The spider emerged from the funnel and headed for the struggling wasp. But the wasp was not really caught at all; it was pretending. As the spider approached, the wasp suddenly advanced toward it, walking on the web as efficiently as the spider itself. The spider realized its mistake and turned to run, but it was too late. The wasp caught it in its mandibles, bent its stinger beneath its own body, and stung the spider, which immediately stopped moving. Then the wasp flew off, carrying the fatally suckered spider.

Unless we manage money carefully, it can turn on us and take control of our lives even to the point of undermining the joy of living. It happened to my artist friend Tom. Tom had established his own freelance art studio and was doing work he loved. He illustrated hundreds of book covers for several American publishers. He made a decent living, which enabled him to raise his family. Then a large publisher offered Tom a high-paying job as an art director. He took it for the big salary. But the job required him to spend most of his time managing the flow of art from his staff of artists and freelancers, attending meetings, dealing with authors' aggressive agents, defending book art to opinionated sales committees, and flying to printing companies to oversee book jacket printing. He made more money but created less art. The job greatly diminished his satisfaction because he found his joy in creating art, not in managing the production of it. Finally, he resigned and returned to freelancing, where he made less money but was much happier.

Escaping the Slavery of Debt

The solution to most of our money problems is quite simple. It is not necessarily to make more money, but rather to maintain control of the money you make so it remains your servant and not your master—a means to an end rather than an end itself. See, I told you it was simple. But simple does not necessarily mean easy. Money can bring out the best or the worst in us, and we must remain vigilant to be sure it is the former.

One of the most insidious pressures on money that prevails in our present culture is the expectation of instant gratification. In today's world, we seldom must wait for anything. We make instant purchases of anything we want with our credit cards. Amazon Prime or FedEx delivers overnight. We download books and internet files in seconds. Do you crave a new car costing tens of thousands of dollars? No need to wait until you save the money; you can get instant credit thirty minutes after you walk into the dealer showroom. Seldom do you need to wait for anything. You can have it right now. So we go into debt not only for a house, but for cars, clothing, furniture, sports, entertainment, or whatever our next whim urges us to buy. As Steve Martin put it, "I love money. I love everything about it. I bought some pretty good stuff. Got me a $300 pair of socks. Got a fur sink. An electric dog polisher. A gasoline-powered turtleneck sweater. And, of course, I bought some dumb stuff, too."

Whatever catches your fancy, you can buy it now and pay later. And pay, and pay, and pay. Debt becomes a form of slavery. You are chained to a contract to pay it all off, and interest accrues as you pay. The mud-dauber has you firmly clenched in its mandibles. Here's how attorney and prominent LDS leader J. Reuben Clark, Jr. described the captivity of paying interest on debt:

> It is a rule . . . in all the world that interest is to be paid on borrowed money. May I say something about interest? Interest never sleeps nor sickens nor dies; it never goes to the hospital; it works on Sundays and holidays; it never takes a vacation; it never visits nor travels . . . it has no love, no sympathy; it is as hard and soulless as a granite cliff. Once in debt, interest is your companion every minute of the day and night; you cannot shun it or slip away from it; you cannot dismiss it; it yields neither to entreaties, demands nor orders; and whenever you get in its way or cross its course or fail to meet its demands, it crushes you.[36]

36 J. Reuben Clark, Jr., Conference Report, April 1938, 103.

How can we avoid the slavery of debt? I offer three simple but effective ways. (Again, simple is not the same as easy. Discipline is required.)

Solution No. 1: Patience. Patience is a form of discipline. Another term for patience is delayed gratification. This means instead of going into debt to buy that thing you want, you wait until you have accumulated the money to buy it. In simpler terms, do not buy until you can afford it. When you are starting out in life, do not look around at what your peers and neighbors have and try to match their excesses. Save, scrimp, do without luxuries. Be frugal in your purchases. Look for bargains. Buy used cars. Shop Walmart instead of Macy's. Do without now so you can have later. As Dave Ramsey put it, "If you will live like no one else, later you can live like no one else." The goal of financial security depends on exercising patience and delaying gratification until the time comes when it is no longer needed. It may help to realize that Warren Buffett made $80 billion of his $86 billion after he was 65 years old.[37]

Solution No. 2: Buy with cash. Of course, there are exceptions to this rule. I do not expect anyone starting out in life to pay cash for a house. Going into debt for houses, real estate, or other appreciating items is usually a sound investment of money. But aside from these rare exceptions, the rule is to avoid debt wherever possible, especially when purchasing depreciating items such as cars. Interest accrues while value declines. As I noted above, exercise the discipline of patience and save until you have the cash to buy.

---

37 "Warren Buffett Has Amassed Over 90% of His Wealth Since He Turned 65," Barron's website: https://www.barrons.com/articles/warren-buffett-has-amassed-over-90-of-his-wealth-since-he-turned-65-51648738715. Accessed September 6, 2023.

When Lanelle and I started our first business, we were determined to avoid debt of any kind. We did not seek an investor to provide our starting capital. We would have owed the investor a return, and we did not want our venture burdened with debt at the outset. For the same reason, we did not take out a bank loan to start the business or a business loan to even out the financial dips. We capitalized our business with money we had saved up. We realized our business was essentially undercapitalized, which would mean slow growth at first. We would have to scrimp and be frugal and live below our means, which we did willingly because we kept our goal of future financial security and independence firmly in our minds.

At first, our business income was uneven. A month of great sales would be followed by a month of almost none. We used the good months to finance the poor ones until we increased sales to where the income leveled out. It worked out well for us. Even through those lean years, we always paid our vendors and met the needs of our family. Soon we began to have money left over that we used to grow the business and invest in other enterprises.

I know that many starting businessmen do seek a lot of startup capital, and it often works well for them. But for me personally, to begin my business in debt would add undue stress to my life, and that would go against my primary philosophy of building a life rather than a business. I wanted my business to serve me and my life goals. I did not want to become a slave to my business.

Solution No. 3: Invest and save. And start doing both as early as possible. Investing in appreciating items is a silent way of growing money. This means investing in real estate, stocks, bonds, etc. By putting money you have earned into investments, it works for you. It becomes your servant. I am reminded of a quote from Albert Einstein that a leader in my church, L. Tom Perry likes to recite about how interest works, "Thems who understand it, earn it. Thems who don't, pay it."

The Payoff: Financial freedom. Mastering your money instead of letting your money master you means freedom from financial worry. It means freedom from the trap of a life spent under the control of money when money becomes the life goal or when we labor under the burden of debt or fail to save and invest for future needs.

According to financial expert Dave Ramsey, "Financial peace isn't the acquisition of stuff. It's learning to live on less than you make, so you can give money back and have money to invest. You can't win until you do this." In his financial peace classes, Ramsey teaches to pay off all debts, live well below your means, save as much as you can, and invest in diversified stocks and bonds and real estate.

Earn It so You Won't Burn It

Malcolm Forbes is quoted as saying, "I made my money the old-fashioned way. I was very nice to a wealthy relative right before he died." J. Paul Getty offered similar advice when he said, "My formula for success is rise early, work late, and strike oil."

These extraordinarily successful entrepreneurs had their tongues firmly planted in their cheeks, of course, but their statements expressed an unfortunate fact: the temptation of getting something for nothing through manipulation or luck seems to be irresistible to many. That is why Americans spend billions buying lottery tickets, playing the odds in casinos, or falling for get-rich-quick schemes. The thought process that spurs these acts usually goes something like this: "If I only had a few thousand more dollars, I could pay off my debts, buy that car I need, and live comfortably without having to scrimp all the time."

But instant-money schemes almost never work. Casinos carefully calculate the odds of their games to favor the house, not the customer. (Think about it: If it were otherwise, they could not stay in business or build those enormous hotels.) The odds of winning a state lottery are millions to one. Yet I hear of people spending high percentages of their weekly paychecks on lottery tickets, not realizing that it increases their odds by such an infinitesimal amount as to be statistically negligible. Even winning a lottery often ruins the life of the winner. The money burns through their pockets like molten magma. They tend to overestimate the extent of their newfound wealth and treat it like Monopoly money, making indulgent purchases, failing to consult financial professionals, falling victim to lifestyle creep, making unwise investments, and lavishly gifting friends and relatives. A high percentage of winners end up broke or even in debt.

For example, Kentucky resident David Edwards won a $27 million jackpot in 2001. He and his wife squandered their fortune on dozens of high-end cars, mansions, and an airplane. A year later they had blown through $12 million and had spiraled into drug addiction. Five years later they were penniless and living in a storage shed. Edwards died alone and broke at age 58.[38]

The problem with unearned money is summed up in the phrase, "easy come, easy go." We do not value what we do not earn. What comes to us at little or no cost tends to depart as quickly as it arrives. On the other hand, we value greatly what we buckle down and earn with our planning, hard work, time, and talent. Knowing the cost makes us appreciate the value. When we put so much of ourselves into what we earn, we protect it and use it with care and

---

38 Andrew Lisa, "23 Lottery Winners Who Lost Millions" Citibank website, July 2023. https://www.gobankingrates.com/net-worth/bankruptcy/lottery-winners-who-lost-millions/

discretion. As the legendary coach Vince Lombardi put it, "The only place where success comes before work is in the dictionary."

Erecting a Foundation of Trust

Trust is the basis of good business. In any business transaction, contract, partnership, or enterprise, trust in the integrity of all parties is the critical key to success. Unfortunately, when money is involved, integrity cannot be taken for granted. We have already noted how the pursuit of money can distort one's values. When that happens, money tends to turn on them like the wasp on the spider and destroy their integrity.

For that reason, it's all the more important that we check out the integrity of those we do business with. Back away if you see anything disturbing at all—even little things such as how they treat and pay their employees and vendors. If their integrity is not active in small things, it will be even worse when it comes to the big things because it's in the big contracts and deals that they'll see opportunity for greater gains, which will put you at greater risk.

Several years ago, when I worked for an advertising special-ty business, I began receiving orders from a business operated by a friend. In time, he suggested that my company should consider using the service his business offered. I thought the reciprocal rela-tionship could benefit both of us, so I agreed. Not long afterward, he requested a quote for some shirts and hats bearing his company logo. I gave him a detailed quote, and he placed the order. After the order was delivered, I sent him an invoice.

My friend paid the invoice, but the check was $8.00 short of the total. I called him to ask why the payment was short, but he did not return my call. Shortly afterward, I received an invoice from his company for a service he had recently performed for my company.

So I called him again and left a message telling him I was about to pay his invoice $8.00 short.

Almost instantly he called back and said, "Hey, what's going on here? Why are you paying my invoice short?"

"Well," I said, "I was just making up for the $8.00 shortage in your payment to me."

He replied, "I shorted your payment because I didn't agree to an $8.00 charge you listed on your invoice."

"But that charge was included in the quote I gave you," I explained, "and you approved the quote." He still refused to pay the $8.00, so I said, "Very well, then I'm not going to do business with you anymore. We will cancel the service you have been offering us."

"But Troy, we're talking about a measly $8.00. Are you really going to sever our business relationship over such a small amount?"

"No," I replied, "I'm not severing the relationship over $8.00. I'm severing it over a loss of trust. If I can't trust you to deal with me fairly over $8.00, how can I trust you when we start dealing in larger amounts? It's best to end it now to prevent the risk of taking a much larger hit later."

As Albert Einstein said, "Whoever is careless with the truth in small matters cannot be trusted with important matters."[39]. Trust is the keystone in the arch of business. Remove it and the whole structure of our economy collapses.

I am happy to say that not all the businessmen I have dealt with are like the person in my story above. To show you the flip side, I will tell you a more heartening story.

---

39 https://www.brainyquote.com/topics/trust-quotes

My first job out of college was a salary-plus-commission sales position. My next job, however, was commission only. I had no salary to fall back on, but the company allowed me to take advance draws against future commissions. By then, Lanelle and I had bought a house and had two little boys. Because it took considerable time to build a clientele sufficient to cover my draw, I soon found myself owing the company $8,000 against commissions I had not yet earned. So, when my next draw check arrived, we said, "We simply cannot accept this. We're going deeper and deeper in debt with each draw." I called the CFO and told him I was returning the check to the company.

The CFO notified the company CEO about the rejection. He called me and wanted to know why I was returning my draw check. I explained my situation: My sales were not covering my draw, and I was going deeper into debt to the company with each check. Furthermore, I had a young, active family and no health insurance, which meant an illness or accident could ruin me financially.

The CEO replied, "Troy, you showed great integrity by returning the check, and I want to find a way to keep people like you. So here's what I'm going to do. The company will provide you with full health insurance for your family. I know you've been working hard, and your sales are growing steadily. I'm confident you will soon be earning your commission and won't even need a draw."

I was overwhelmed. As it turned out, the CEO's words were prophetic. My sales skyrocketed immediately, and soon I was able to pay back my $8,000 debt and earn for myself and the company multiple times their cost in paying my insurance. It was a great example of how integrity exhibited by both parties can cause results to multiply exponentially.

This is a lesson the young billionaire needed to learn in the movie *Beauty and the Billionaire*. In acquiring a business for his conglomerate, the billionaire played hardball with the company's CEO, agreeing to terms he did not intend to honor and ruining her reputation when she resisted his bulldozing takeover tactics. When confronted with his duplicity and wrecking-ball measures, he dismissed his actions as "just good business." I hear that phrase all too often. Doing whatever it takes to make a profit is dismissed as "just good business." That is not true, as the billionaire learned later when he tried to negotiate another deal with the same CEO, and she would have nothing to do with him.

There seems to be a general consensus that truth, honesty, and integrity are fast disappearing from American culture. I do not know if this is true, but if it is, it means conducting your own business with honesty and integrity provides you with a real opportunity for success. When you are honest in your dealings while the world around you is not, it makes doing business with you much more attractive because people will trust you. You will stand out from your competitors, and customers are more likely to flock to your door. That is one reason why building a good reputation for honesty and integrity is so important. It is one of the most valuable assets you can acquire.

The Exponential Rewards of Giving

In the classic musical comedy *Hello Dolly*, the half-a-millionaire Horace Vandergelder says, "Money, pardon the expression, is like manure. It's not worth a thing unless it's spread around, encouraging young things to grow."

Though his metaphor was a little crude, this successful businessman understood something about the use of money that is easy to lose sight of. Money is not to be hoarded. To succeed exponentially we must share our wealth in ways that benefit others.

It has happened to me many times, and I have lost count of how many times I've heard from others how when they gave generously, they soon found unexpected benefits pouring back to them. It is a reality principle. Giving money is like planting seeds: You reap far more than you sow.

An experience shared by my friend Troy Anderson illustrates the principle. Troy's wife came down with severe COVID pneumonia, which led to several additional life-threatening conditions. She was hospitalized for seventeen days, and the doctors gave her only a fifty-fifty chance of survival. But, through prayer and superb medical care, she recovered and was eventually released to go home. Troy was extremely grateful, but he now encountered a new challenge: a hospital bill of over $150,000 for expenses insurance would not cover.

Troy applied for relief through several agencies but was turned down because he made too much money. So he applied to the Presbyterian hospital that had treated his wife, hoping for a discount. He lost hope when they asked for his tax returns, lists of his assets, properties, and every detail of his financial standing. They would see clearly that he was not destitute.

But to Troy's great surprise and utter elation, the hospital forgave the bill entirely. He was "blown away," as he put it. He still does not know why they forgave the bill, but his best guess is that in his financial records they saw the extent of his giving to churches and charities, and they decided to "pay it forward,"—to pass the generosity along.

Troy's story is a perfect example of what Jesus promised to the generous: His gift returned to him in full, pressed down, shaken together to make room for more, running over, and poured into his lap. Generous giving is another way of excelling exponentially. As Winston Churchill said, "We make a living by what we get, but we make a life by what we give."

Lanelle and I recently took a trip to Israel, and there I found in the very geography of the land a superb example of the difference between giving and hoarding. We visited the Sea of Galilee, which is really a large, freshwater lake where many events in the life of Jesus and his disciples occurred. That lake is fed by the Jordan River coming into it from the north. The Jordan River flows outward at the south end of the lake and continues southward until it empties into the Salt Sea.

The waters of the Sea of Galilee are continually fresh and pure because they are continually renewed by the inflow and outflow. Fish thrive in the lake, its water is drinkable, and greenery abounds on its shores. But the Salt Sea, which receives the water given to it by the Sea of Galilee, has no outlet. The water that flows into it stays and becomes salty and undrinkable. Nothing can live in the Salt Sea or on its shores, which is why it is known more commonly by its more dreadful name—the Dead Sea. I found these two seas to be graphic examples of the difference between giving and hoarding. It is the difference between life and death. (By the way, I cannot float in water, but I could float in the Dead Sea because of the salt content of the water. If you ever go there, try it for yourself. It is enchanting.)

It is always important to remember that money is never the key to happiness or a good life. Often the happiest people are those who have very little money. Wage-earners living in three-bedroom tract homes, driving five-year-old Chevys, shopping at thrift stores, and dedicated to their families and churches are often among the most contented people you will find. But even for them, the solid principles of avoiding debt, saving, and living below one's means spell the difference between financial slavery and financial freedom. That is why I say that, though money is not the key to happiness, managing money wisely, both in business and in one's personal life, is a vital key to excelling exponentially.

Exert Effort with Energy and Enthusiasm

"Productivity is never an accident. It is always the result of a commitment to excellence, intelligent planning, and focused effort."

—Paul J. Meyer

"Friendship, love, health, energy, enthusiasm, and joy are the things that make life worth living and exploring."

—Denise Austin

A colleague of mine—I'll call him Jack—told me of an incident that occurred when he was stopped at a traffic light in the left-turn lane adjacent to the center median. A man bearing a cardboard sign tapped his window and asked for a handout.

Jack fished out a five-dollar bill, rolled down his window, and gave it to the beggar. He took it in his fingers and said crossly, "Man, is that the best you can do? Surely you can spare me a twenty. I can't feed my family on five-dollar bills." Feeling a little angry at this display of ingratitude, Jack tried to pull the bill back, but the beggar quickly jerked it away. Jack rolled up his window and drove on.

I view this incident as an example of a scourge that is spreading across our nation—a growing sense of unearned entitlement. The street beggar apparently felt that because he had a need and Jack had money, he was entitled to a share of it. But he had not earned the right to a share of Jack's assets, and Jack was not obligated to share them with an unknown recipient. For one thing, Jack could not be sure the man was being truthful. Many street beggars are con men perfectly capable of working. Yet Jack made it a habit of giving a modest amount to street beggars solely on the chance that their need might be real. Even so, he felt no obligation to feed the beggar's entire family (if he really had one). He saw his smaller donation as merely one of many that the beggar would accumulate to meet his family's needs.

Now, it is true that we who have should be charitably generous to those who have nothing or little, but Jack felt that he had the right and responsibility to decide for himself the best ways to distribute his charitable contributions. He was not willing to let a stranger's sense of undue entitlement rule his decisions.

When you define entitlement correctly, there is no problem with it. It simply means your right to have what you have earned or what is rightfully yours. The problem arises when one feels a sense of entitlement or of being owed something he has done little or nothing to earn. It is the expectation of reward without corresponding effort.

Think about it and you will realize that there is no such thing as a reward that requires no effort. You may say, "Oh yes there is. There are birthday and Christmas presents, and the favor someone does for you out of the goodness of their heart. How about the guy who won a huge prize of season tickets to his favorite team's basketball games just by purchasing a raffle ticket?" Well, the guy may have gotten the reward free, but the sponsoring company had to pay for those tickets with money earned by the efforts of its employees. The same holds true for any gift; you reap the free result of what someone else earned, but the earning had to be done to pay for the gift and make it available. The point is, anytime there is a reward, someone puts in the effort to earn it. The entitlement mentality does not eliminate the requirement of effort to produce a reward; it simply expects a reward that results from someone else's effort.

To show how this concept plays out in the workplace, let me relate to you an example from my own experience. For months, I had been exercising, and I thought I was in pretty good shape. Lanelle and I were preparing to travel to Oklahoma to check on our business when she turned to me and asked, "Troy, can you do 100 push-ups?"

"All at once?" I replied, a little apprehensively.

"No, not all at once. Ten at a time, with a little breather between each set."

"Well, of course," I said with my typical machismo. Had I realized what she had in mind, I might have claimed to have a sprained shoulder.

What Lanelle had in mind was a unique exercise to demonstrate to our employees that their profit share depends on the success of our company, which in turn depends on the mutual effort of every worker. She wanted to show that if one does not pull his own weight, others have to take up the slack.

At our weekly team meeting, nine of our employees came into the conference room where Lanelle had brought in ten freshly made cheesecakes from the local bakery. She turned to the first employee and said, "Kelly, would you like a cheesecake?"

When Kelly enthusiastically said "yes," Lanelle turned to me and said, "Troy, would you do ten push-ups so Kelly can have a cheesecake?"

"Sure," I said, and immediately I dropped to the floor and did ten push-ups.

Lanelle then turned to the next employee. "Wendy, would you like a cheesecake?"

Wendy also wanted a cheesecake, so I was asked to do ten more push-ups so Wendy could have one. This went on for another employee or so, then as they began to realize what was going on, the yesses became more hesitant. Then came the first "no." The employee turned down the cheesecake because she did not want to put me through another set of push-ups. But as it turned out, her empathy was wasted.

Lanelle turned to me and said, "Troy, since Bobbi doesn't want a cheesecake, will you do ten push-ups because we've already bought one for her?" So I fell to the floor and did another ten.

By then, I had done sixty to seventy push-ups. I was sweating like a squeezed sponge, breathing hard, and my push-ups had become embarrassingly slower. But Lanelle had no pity. She continued around the table and offered a cheesecake to the remaining employees, and regardless of their answer, I had to do ten more push-ups. When all the employees thought we were finally done, they expressed empathetic relief. They hated the idea that someone was having to work so hard to provide the cheesecakes. They felt guilty eating a cheesecake provided by someone else's hard work. But it was not quite over. Lanelle looked at the remaining cheesecakes and said, "I believe I want a cheesecake. Troy, would you do ten more push-ups so I can have one?" So with triceps screaming and sweat pouring, I struggled through my one-hundredth push-up. My muscles were sore for a week.

After it was all over (and I was thinking about calling for a stretcher to carry me out), Lanelle made the point: The reward of profit share is based on the success of the company, and the success of the company is based on the individual effort of all employees pulling (or maybe in this case, pushing up) their own weight. When an employee slacks off or calls in sick when he is not, other employees have to fill in. They must work harder so the slacking employee can have a share of the reward he did not fully earn. All must exert the effort so the rewards can be fairly distributed among all employees. The failure of some to exert the effort needed to succeed means they are freeriding on the effort of others.

Exerting Effort is not an Option: It's a Necessity

If you are looking for an easy path to excellence, you are living on the wrong planet. That path does not exist here on the third rock from the Sun. Ever since our first parents were expelled from the Garden of Eden, nothing worthwhile has come easy for us. We contend with the Second Law of Thermodynamics, which says everything is moving toward greater disorder, or in a nutshell, that things are inevitably running down. We contend with nature—droughts, storms, earthquakes, floods, vermin, decay, parasites. We contend with the human factor—opposition, dishonesty, misunderstanding, slothful help. And we contend with ourselves—our health, energy levels, lack of knowledge, propensity for mistakes, and negative personality traits. It's all summed up in Murphy's Law, which says, "If anything can go wrong, it will."

Wow! With all that working against us, it is a wonder we ever get anything done. That is why we who want to excel exponentially must decide up front to expend the needed effort to accomplish our goals. But deciding up front is not the same as deciding once and for all. As my friend Tom tells me, he is very good at getting organized, but he's terrible at staying organized. Many of us have good starting power, but it is the staying power—our endurance, the commitment to continued effort—that makes the ultimate difference. Those forces working against us are forever active, and we must resolve to renew our effort to challenge them every morning the moment our feet hit the floor.

The problem with exerting effort is that it takes a lot of... well... effort. It is a word that implies hard work, expending energy, getting tired, pushing past limits, and sacrificing time and pleasure in favor of responsibility and duty. It means swimming upstream, taking the hard road, and keeping our nose to the grindstone. Where do we find the will and the stick-to-itiveness to keep plugging away when more seems to be required than we have to give? I offer four keys to help us keep exerting effort when we're tempted to give in.

Four Keys to Maintaining Sufficient Effort

Key No. 1: Focus on the ultimate goal. This means keeping the main thing the main thing. Do not chase every squirrel that crosses your path. Keep your ultimate goal before you as you work through the individual parts of any difficult task. Visualize the finished product or condition that will exist when all the individual parts are completed.

A group of amateur mountain climbers hired a veteran guide to take them to the peak of a Colorado mountain. As they approached the base of the mountain, the guide stopped the climbers and pointed to the snow-capped peak, gleaming in the morning sunlight. He said to them, "I want you to take a long look at the peak of our mountain. That is our goal, and you need to get its image firmly lodged in your mind because when you begin climbing, you will no longer be able to see the top. You will be forced to concentrate on the rocky surface in front of you, looking for handholds and footholds in outcroppings and crevasses. Your legs and arms will ache with exhaustion and your fingers will become raw from gripping the flinty rocks. The hard work of climbing may discourage you and make you want to turn back unless you keep the vision of your goal firmly in mind." That guide's advice described a pivotal key to the success of any endeavor you tackle.

Key No. 2: Identify your reason for working. If you are working on a dull, repetitive task with no glamorous end result—like sweeping floors or manning an assembly line station—find the true reason you are doing the job. Usually there is more than one. First, you were hired to do it, so your integrity means you must perform the task to the best of your ability. You can take pride in doing even the most mundane job well. It reflects who you are. Second, remember the biblical parable of the talents, which tells us that he who excels in small things earns the right to do greater things. Doing mundane tasks well earns the respect of supervisors and can lead to promotions. (I will say more about this later.) Or maybe the primary reason you took the job is simply to feed your family. That alone is a high purpose that should motivate you to put forth whatever effort is required.

The vice president of a large American publishing company tells the story of his father, who spent his entire working life at an Ohio manufacturing plant making airplane tires. The son asked his father how he found satisfaction in doing the same repetitive task every day of his forty-year working career. The father replied, "I found plenty of satisfaction in my job. My work provided everything I needed to raise my family."

Key No. 3: Express gratitude. Being grateful for your job can provide a strong motivation to exert effort, even if the job is not high-paying or glamorous.

A friend described to me his experience when he visited with a vendor whose companies outsourced menial work such as sorting, hand-packaging, product inspecting, etc. The work was menial and repetitive, and the company hired only disabled workers who were generally incapable of complex tasks. All were impaired, some physically, some mentally, and some in both ways. Yet the company was known for high quality and extreme accuracy. My friend was impressed by the extraordinary diligence of these workers. All of them threw themselves into their work, totally focused, very industrious, never flagging, and always cheerful. He asked the manager how he managed to motivate his workers to be so diligent. The manager replied, "I don't have to motivate them at all. Every one of them is grateful to have work. Grateful for a place where their activity and effort have meaning. It's their gratitude that generates the enthusiasm and effort you are witnessing."

Several times throughout my career I have had the opportunity to donate my time to a local charitable organization. It was a food cannery that canned and shipped food to alleviate hunger across the world. Although the work was mundane, repetitive, and hot, it truly gave me a sense of gratification that comes from helping others. It also made me grateful for my own job, even though it too was sometimes mundane and repetitive.

Key No. 4: Realize the value of your work. You may have graduated from school with high hopes of being the chief executive of a multi-billion-dollar corporation, a high-ranking elected official, or a famous actor or singer. Instead, you are working for a salary in a cubicle or clerking in a law office or driving a delivery truck. It is commendable to aspire to high pinnacles, but while we are aspiring, we must realize that openings at the top are very rare. The economy needs only a few CEOs, governors, or movie stars, but there is always a need for the millions of workers to fill the cubicles, man the sales floors, keep the computers running, and process the paperwork. It is these unheralded jobs that are the backbone of the national economy. They keep the nation running, and the economy cannot do without them. Even the smallest, most menial task is necessary. So remember, no matter how small and insignificant your job may seem to you, it is vital to keep the wheels of industry turning. To maintain the effort needed to excel at your job, pat yourself on the back for doing your part to keep our nation economically strong.

There is also another benefit to putting out effort even on a mundane job. In this age of entitlement, many workers apply whatever effort it takes to get by. When you put forth full-throttle effort, you will stand out among your fellow workers. Management will notice, and your diligence will greatly increase your chances of being moved up to a higher position.

Enthusiasm Generates Effort

One of my favorite Bible characters is the Apostle Peter. And often he really was a character! Peter was irrepressible—even ebullient. He was eager to try things, the first to venture out, to take risks, to dare the odds. He saw Jesus walking on water, and he had to try it. He saw Jesus on the beach, and when the boat moved too slow for him, he jumped in and swam ashore. When Jesus was threatened, Peter drew his sword and started swinging.

I like Peter. He had that "gung-ho, let's get at it" attitude that can propel people to do great things—if channeled properly. And that was sometimes Peter's problem. His enthusiasm often got ahead of his judgment. After walking toward Jesus on the water, he took his eye off the mark and focused instead on the waves, which caused him to sink. After wounding a man with his wildly swinging sword, Jesus had to admonish him to put his weapon away, for his brash attack did not follow the plan of God.

But when Peter tamed his enthusiasm and put it in service of his ultimate goal, he became the most successful of Jesus' original followers. He was the acknowledged leader of the newly founded church and the hero of the first half of the Bible's book of Acts.

Applying enthusiasm effectively involves a delicate balancing act. What you want is not to curb your enthusiasm, but to direct it. Yes, you must put reins on it, but the purpose of the reins—like those we place on a horse—is not to stifle enthusiasm but to direct it toward your goal. As Ralph Waldo Emerson said, "Enthusiasm is the mother of effort, and without it nothing great was ever achieved."

The Transfer of Enthusiasm

My enthusiasm for football began when I was about eight years old. I brought home a paper for my mom to sign that would certify her approval for me to play Little League football. After I handed her the paper, she looked it over and said, "What if I don't sign it?" I replied, "Then I will go get some other mom to sign it." She signed it.

Throughout my grade school and high school years, I remained enthusiastic about football. I even loved the grueling practice sessions. Practicing was not a chore for me because I enjoyed every minute of it—well, maybe except for the times I got injured.

That kind of enthusiasm tends to be contagious. When a motivational speaker, coach, boss, or salesperson is enthusiastic about his product or service, it usually incites his listeners to act. They want whatever he is selling. This is called the "transfer of enthusiasm," a term coined by sales expert and motivational speaker, Brian Tracy. The enthusiasm is transmitted from the one who has it to those who would benefit from using his product or service. The point is your enthusiasm can infect others around you and help your company, your team, or your job to excel exponentially.

The Reward for Effort and Enthusiasm

The reward for effort and enthusiasm is accomplishment—the accomplishment of difficult things and even so-called impossible things. How many things can you think of that we have today that were once considered impossible? Before the invention of the steam engine less than two centuries ago, it was thought impossible that a vehicle could move without horses. In my grandfather's childhood, it was thought that man would never fly. In my father's childhood, it was thought man would never travel to the moon. If you told someone in 1973, when the first cell phone was made, that in a few decades, almost everyone would carry in their pockets a tiny device with many times more power than all the combined computers NASA used to put men on the moon, no one would have taken you seriously.

People with vision who were willing to put forth the effort have accomplished great things. As the above examples show, very few things are really impossible. I am reminded of this little poem by Edgar A. Guest called "It Couldn't Be Done", quoted here in condensed form:

Somebody said it couldn't be done,
    But he with a chuckle replied
That "maybe it couldn't," but he would be one
    Who wouldn't say so till he'd tried.
So he buckled right in with the trace of a grin
    And if ever he worried he hid it. ...
He started to sing as he tackled the thing
    That couldn't be done, and he did it.

Energetic effort and enthusiasm result in accomplishment, and accomplishment offers more than one reward. Not only do you get the new or improved thing or condition that exists as a result of your effort, but you also get the validation of yourself as a person of worth. You have applied your abilities, you have made a difference, you have left a mark, you have fulfilled a purpose and thus given your life a sense of meaning in the accomplishment of something worthwhile.

And that, my patient reader, is what this little book has been about. We who are in business or who work for a paycheck will not find joy or fulfillment in our work if we think of it solely as a way to make money. Throughout these pages, I have tried to impress upon you the idea that the true business of life consists of more than just the bottom line of the balance sheet, the value of your stocks and bonds, or the expansion of your bank account. The true goal of life is to achieve excellence not merely in business but in all the areas of life that give it true meaning.

The overarching truth that runs through this book is that *fulfillment in life comes through how we treat and serve others.* Remember what the ghost of Marley learned too late. As he said when he warned Scrooge to change his ways, "Mankind was my business!"

The English poet John Donne put it this way: "No man is an island." We are all connected to each other and dependent on each other. We all need help sometimes, which means we all must be ready to provide help and service to others when their needs arise. We work to acquire the resources needed to render this kind of help. Our companies provide income not only for ourselves but for others as well—our employees, their families, our suppliers, and our clients. In turn, the paychecks or products they receive enable them to benefit those in their own environments. The good we do by our efforts radiates outward and affects others, who in turn affect others, who in turn affect others, *ad infinitum.*

When you view your work in your company or at your job with this perspective, you are sure to excel in life because you live fully in all your areas of activity—your work, your home, your recreation, your relationships, and your church. This is true excellence because it never stops multiplying. It is exponential. It multiplies by giving you a life filled with the achievement of joy, peace, happiness, freedom, and contentment—a life of excellence that is sure to produce rewards exponentially in your life and in the lives of those whom you touch.

EPILOGUE

Exponential Experimentation

In this book, I have given you eleven chapters, each introducing an essential element that will help you excel exponentially in all areas of life. However, embedded within these eleven chapters are references to seven additional elements that are also important aids to achieving excellence. They tend to orbit around or support in various ways the eleven elements that are the primary focus of the chapters.

These 18 elements are based on eternal principles. They were already in place and operative 888 years ago, and they will still be around 888 years from now. By employing all of them together, you will not only excel but excel exponentially. As you know by now, excelling exponentially means living a life filled with joy, peace, happiness, freedom, and contentment.

As you have read this book, I hope you were able to extract all of these essential elements. To help you in that quest, in this epilogue, I offer you a comprehensive list of all the eighteen elements addressed either overtly or subtly in the book, along with suggested exercises to help you put each of the principles into practice.

The Eighteen Essential Elements to be Employed

1. Extraordinary

Realize and accept that you are extraordinary. No one in world history has been exactly like you. Your gifts, talents, interests, and outlooks are unique to you alone. That means you have something to give to your community or the world that nobody else has. Find that uniqueness and put it into action. It is a key to excelling exponentially. You are extraordinary because you are a child of God, as is every other person!

2. Expectations

Is it possible that you are not excelling because your expectations are too low? Call up the courage to reach a little higher. That unreachable star may not be unreachable after all.

3. Education

Education is a vital key to excellence. It is critical that you continue to enhance your education throughout life. Selective and consistent reading, attending seminars, or taking online classes are ways of continuing your education.

4. Exercise

Your body is your primary home, and to keep it healthy enough to live in requires care. This means regular exercise as well as a proper diet. Your other personal endowments—mental, spiritual, and social—also require regular attention, assessment, and exercise to remain healthy and functional. Regular exercise in all these areas requires discipline and intentionality. You must resist the natural pull to slack up.

5. Examples

Good examples encourage us. We need heroes to emulate. They inspire us by showing what is possible. They achieved their goal, so it is likely that you can too. Actively search for examples who can inspire you to do better, reach higher, and keep looking up.

6. Environment

Good environments are critical to success. If your work, home, or personal environments are less than optimal, uncover the problem, whether its employees, unresolved issues, inattention to needs, or even some blind spot of your own. Once uncovered, take positive steps to correct it.

7. Emotions

Emotions show that we are human and not machines. But emotions can get out of hand. To control them, we must strive for stable relationships and productive work environments that encourage positive emotions and discourage negative ones.

8. Empathy

The ability to put yourself in the shoes of a troubled person is an essential element to success in business or personal relationships. It is a trait that can be cultivated through relating someone's problems to your own experience or using your imagination to understand their feelings.

9. Ethics

Good ethics are indispensable to exponential excellence. In today's environment of declining honesty and integrity, a reputation for good ethical practices will make your business and your life stand out from the rest. You will be respected and much more likely to succeed.

10. Etiquette

The point of etiquette is not just which fork to use or how you eat your soup. It is using proper manners on all occasions, ensuring that those in your environment feel at ease. Etiquette and mannerly behavior must become ingrained within our psyche like a habit. It must become part of who we are, so that the self we present to others is not just an act but reflects the reality of who we are.

11. Effort

Excellence or success never "just happens." It is always the result of effort. Choose a business and a life path that you can throw yourself into with eagerness and joy, and then put all your effort into making it work, and you will excel exponentially.

12. Enthusiasm

A "gung-ho, let's get at it" attitude can propel you to do great things—if channeled properly. Enthusiasm must be managed, or it can get ahead of judgment. Using enthusiasm effectively involves a delicate balancing act. The trick is not to curb it but to direct it toward your goal.

13. Economics

Earn it before you spend it. That's the key to exponential excellence in economics. Borrowing to purchase anything other than appreciating assets, or depending on chance factors for financial success is a sure path to economic disaster. Money can be an asset or a trap. The key is to learn to use it wisely so you will be its master instead of letting it master you.

14. Energy

George MacDonald (a literary mentor to C. S. Lewis) tells the story of a young heroine on a quest who is directed to enter a deep hole in the ground. "But there are no stairs," she pro-tests. "You must throw yourself in," replied her guide. "There is no other way."[40] Our quest for excellence calls for the same directive. We must throw ourselves into whatever we do with energy and enthusiasm. Whether it is your workplace, family, or any other endeavor, there is no substitute for giving it all the energy you have. Your energy and enthusiasm will positively infect the others in your environment.

The Encumbering Elements that are Essential to Eliminate

The remainder of the list includes negative elements, or encumbrances to achieving excellence. Encumbrances are dead weights that can slow us down or hold us back. They are like choking weeds in a garden. Find them and root them out of your life so you and your business can grow to their full potential.

15. Envy

Envy is an unproductive and unhappy emotion caused by the desire for something possessed by another. Two keys to overcoming envy are (1) learning to be happy with what one has (contentment), and (2) striving to earn what you want instead of envying the person who has it. Envy only hurts you, not the person you are envious of. Most likely the other person does not know you are envious of him or her.

16. Ego

Ego focuses on oneself, which overshadows concern for others. Ego inflates one's own abilities and thus blinds him to the need to correct flaws and improve. Ego damages relationships and

---

40 George MacDonald, "The Golden Key," in *The Gifts of the Child Christ* (Grand Rapids MI: Wm. B. Eerdmans, 1996).

can drive away clients. Ego must be conquered and subdued if one is to excel exponentially.

17. Excuses

The day you stop making excuses for your failures will be the day you take full responsibility for yourself and your actions and begin to excel exponentially. Those who take full responsibility for their actions exhibit nobility, courage, and a high sense of personal responsibility.

18. Enemies

Your competitors are not your enemies. Competition spurs diligence. Enemies are any who try to prevent or discourage you from pursuing excellence. Identify them and avoid them or refuse to listen to their input. Take care not to fall into habits that make you your own worst enemy.

Three Keys to Making the Essential Elements Work for You

1. Exercise the Elements

To excel exponentially, you must do more than just read about these essential elements; you must employ them in your life every day. Reading about excellence will not achieve it. It must be put into action (and as Arturo Toscanini said, that means "practice, practice, practice"). You need to experiment with these elements, learn how to apply them effectively, and make them a part of your everyday life.

2. Entwine the Elements

One difficulty in writing chapters on these individual elements is that after introducing each and demonstrating how it works, I must then move on from chapter to chapter without explaining one critical factor involved in their application. That factor is this: To be effective, these separate elements must not remain separated. They are not designed to work in isolation from each other. They must work together in tandem, each feeding and enhancing the others in ways that make their combined power exponentially greater than the sum of their individual applications.

For example, consider the fingers of your hand. Each finger is relatively weak by itself. But when they work together as a unit, they accomplish goals each would be incapable of individually—as they do when they form a powerful vise to grip a hammer or a baseball bat, or to make a fist to pound a punching bag. By working together, they become extremely effective instruments.

Each of the elements in this book will enhance your life and business and help you to excel. Education will help you excel; ethics will help you excel; as will using good etiquette, empathy, and effort. But practice all these elements together, and they will interact with each other. Each will feed, support, and enhance all the others, and it will be like an explosion of excellence in your life and business. You will not merely excel; you will excel exponentially.

3. **Embody the Elements**

My third and final point to leave you with is this: To really work and be effective, the elements in this book cannot simply be attachments that you put on or leave off at will. They do not work well if you use them only when convenient or needed and then put them away the rest of the time. They must be internalized. They must become part of you in ways that define who you are all the time. They are not like a good suit of clothes you wear only on Sunday. They must become absorbed into your life if they are to have real meaning and be effective. We must do more than just practice them; we must live them.

I remember one of the first business trips I took with a senior vice president of the company I once worked for. I had looked up to this man. He seemed to employ ethics and empathy. But one evening, when I was riding in a car with him, his demeanor and language changed drastically. His conversation was no longer gentlemanly and circumspect. It was peppered with the worst kind of profanity and offensive subjects. I was greatly surprised and disappointed to find that he was not the same person in private that he presented himself to be on the job. He lost my respect because he demonstrated that his disciplined and ethical demeanor was merely a mask that hid the real person inside.

No mask can hide the truth forever. It will eventually slip, revealing the truth behind it. That is why it is so critically important to be what you present yourself to be. Adopt into your life these eighteen essential elements for living and working, and you will develop an integrated personality—that is, a personality that reflects integrity in all its facets. That, my friend, will enable you to excel exponentially.

My Epiphany

The term *excel* is defined as "to surpass others or be superior in some respect or area; do extremely well, outdo." This is a good definition, but my only problem with it is that it makes it seem like excelling is a competition rather than a life-enhancing practice. We do not want to excel simply to be better than our neighbors or coworkers; we want to excel because it creates the best possible life for us and those in our environments.

As I thought more about this idea, however, I realized that there is one sense in which we would all enjoy trying to outdo others. What if we all tried to outdo each other in being more loving, joyful, kind, peaceful, content, compassionate, courageous, trustworthy, honest, loyal, helpful, friendly, positive, encouraging, patient, reverent, clean, cheerful, brave, courteous, obedient, forgiving, understanding, caring, engaging, thrifty, prayerful, virtuous, true, chaste, civil, and benevolent? Now that is a competition that would make all of us winners. It would create the kind of world we would all enjoy living in—a world in which everyone would excel in virtue and care for others. That, my dear and patient reader, is excelling exponentially.

ABOUT THE AUTHOR

Troy Butterfield is a successful real estate investor and businessman. In partnership with his wife, Lanelle, the couple has specialized in growing, managing, and selling small businesses. Their past businesses include promotional products and property management companies, and they presently own and operate a service business called Color and Relationships, which helps businesses and families find peace and profit through better personal and employer-employee relationships.

Troy and Lanelle have been married for thirty-six years and counting.. They raised four sons (Lanelle insists that she really had five boys to deal with). Their family has expanded to include two daughters-in-law and two grandsons. They love to travel and have set foot in thirty-one of the United States and over twenty-five foreign countries. A man of deep faith and patriotism, Troy loves to talk about two subjects no one is supposed to mention—religion and politics.

Despite his achievements in his personal life and businesses, Troy considers himself to be "just an average sort of guy." Yet he always wanted his life to make a difference—to mean something more than just trudging through the motions of making a decent living. By reading, observing, and emulating good examples, he built his own life around a set of solid principles which he calls "Essential Elements." These elements enabled him to rise above mediocrity and achieve exponential excellence. After watching so many friends, colleagues, and business acquaintances struggle to find peace and contentment, Troy felt a strong need to share with others his elemental discoveries in what it takes to achieve exponential excellence. The result is this book, *Excel Exponentially*.

Want more? Scan the QR code below and gain VIP access to Troy's latest news, inspiring resources, and exclusive updates!